THE GARDENS AT
HATFIELD

THE GARDENS AT HATFIELD

SUE SNELL

with an introduction by
The Dowager Marchioness of Salisbury

FRANCES LINCOLN

Frances Lincoln Limited
4 Torriano Mews, Torriano Avenue
London NW5 2RZ
www.franceslincoln.com

The Gardens at Hatfield
Copyright © Frances Lincoln Limited 2005
Introduction text
copyright © The Dowager Marchioness of Salisbury 2005
Foreword and captions to the photographs
copyright © Sue Snell 2005
Photographs copyright © Sue Snell 2005
except for those on the following pages:
The Bodleian Library, University of Oxford:
13 left (MS Ashmole 1461, fol. 141r)
13 right (MS Ashmole 1461, fol. 29r)
By courtesy of The Marquess of Salisbury:
10, 11, 12, 14, 15, 17, 18, 19, 21, 26, 43
Plan of the gardens copyright © Jean Sturgis 2005

First Frances Lincoln edition 2005

A catalogue record for this book is
available from the British Library.

Designed by Becky Clarke

Printed and bound in China

ISBN 0 7112 2516 8
9 8 7 6 5 4 3 2

LOVE AND THANKS TO PETER DAVIES

Endpapers Bird's-eye view of the House and
Gardens at Hatfield by artist Marcus May
Half-title page An Italian stone fruit basket
at the foot of the steps leading from the
East Parterre to the Box Walk
Title page Hatfield House and the Gardens
from the far side of the New Pond
These pages Spring blossom in the Orchard

CONTENTS

FOREWORD

by Sue Snell

This book is a photographic journey, my story in images taken in the gardens of Hatfield House, Hertfordshire. It is a tribute to a great garden and its creators.

My very first visit to the house was on one of those perfect summer days which start hazy and misty early in the morning and become sunny and hot well before noon. I loved the gardens instantly, and I continue to do so at all times of the gardening year, especially in winter on bright, cold, icy days when the wrapped stone figures stand motionless against the sky, ice on the pond has to be broken so that ducks and geese can swim, and rabbit tracks can be found in the snow.

I was first introduced to the sixth Marchioness of Salisbury in 1998, by plantswoman and photographer Valerie Finnis. Lady Salisbury generously gave me an open invitation to explore and photograph the gardens at Hatfield, which she had been so imaginatively restoring and developing since she and her husband took up residence there in 1972. It has been a great privilege to explore these historic gardens and fascinating to record the innovations and changes to the design, structure and planting undertaken by Lady Salisbury together with the Head Gardener, David Beaumont, and his gardeners.

Fifty-six acres of gardens surround Hatfield House. They spill out into the 7,000 acres of the Park, parterres and knot gardens framed in dark green and filled with a profusion of flowers, radiating from the house as points of the compass, North, South, East and West.

I love taking spontaneous images, always working with natural light. I photograph as I find, searching for the unexpected and unusual: hidden landscapes, people and their lives, animals, bold vistas under ever-varying skies, small details of tiny plants and secret corners.

Today, in the Textile Conservation rooms hidden in the roof, specialist needlewomen, working much as their predecessors did, restore rare embroideries and tapestries. Often the needlework is decorated with flowers that grew at Hatfield when the gardens were created and that flourish there again today. It is this way in which people, plants and place come together at Hatfield that has intrigued me.

The Rainbow portrait of Queen Elizabeth I in the house, attributed to Isaac Oliver (1565–1617), shows the Queen wearing a bodice embroidered with wild flowers. In her reign plants held a great symbolism and were used extensively in both painting and embroidery.

The first Earl of Salisbury, who built the impressive Jacobean structure, commissioned the French garden designer Salomon de Caus and employed John Tradescant the Elder as gardener and plant-hunter. It was Tradescant who was sent to Flanders with £10 to acquire 16,000 vines for the Vineyard

of which Samuel Pepys wrote in his diary entry for 22 July 1661, 'So by degrees till I come to Hatfield before twelve o'clock and walked all alone to the Vineyard which is now a very beautiful place again, and coming back I met with Mr. Locker, my Lord's gardener . . .' The Vineyard, private and discreetly tucked away in the Park, is still 'a very beautiful place'.

When Lady Salisbury's husband died in 2003, she began to make plans to leave her gardens and her friends, and it seemed an appropriate time to publish my images. The emotional framework of a gardener's life is often represented by the flow and form of their gardens, and nowhere is this more evident than at Hatfield. In her introduction to this book Lady Salisbury reveals her love of the gardens as she records both their history and her own personal story of how she reworked them. I hope I have captured and recorded this in my photographs.

Above Lady Salisbury's dog, Bonnie
Centre Dark red tulip 'Black Parrot'
Below Specialist needlewomen of the Textile Conservation Group, working on a rare seventeenth-century embroidery in rooms high up at the top of the house overlooking the West Garden

INTRODUCTION

by The Dowager Marchioness of Salisbury

In recorded time, the story of the gardens at Hatfield begins in the early years of the seventeenth century, but my imagination plays with the idea that the tale could have begun forty years earlier, with the seeds of their creation being sown in the mind of a young boy with an acute brain and a crooked body. He plays in a paradise garden amongst the scents of pinks and roses, splashes in the sparkling waters of the fountains, teases and feeds the fish, climbs to the top of the mount and rolls down its grassy slope, and loses himself in the mysterious paths of the maze. The boy was Robert Cecil, second son of Lord Burghley, Lord Treasurer to Queen Elizabeth. A fantasy yes, but how often is a love of gardening born in childhood, and Robert's love for it might well have stemmed from the carefree days spent in his father's garden at Theobalds in Hertfordshire. Theobalds when Burghley bought it in 1563 was a simple manor, but over the years he enlarged it, writing that it was 'Begun by me with a mean measure, but increased by Her Majesty often coming.'

The increases were immense: so considerable that, by the time he had finished enlarging it, the manor was, except for Hampton Court Palace and the Palace of Westminster, the largest building in England. Visitors were astonished, not only by the Palace but also by its gardens, with their fountains and mazes, the statues of the Caesars and its moated garden.

On Burghley's death in 1598 Robert inherited Theobalds, but he was not to keep it long. In 1603, on his progress from Scotland to claim his new kingdom, King James stayed at Theobalds. This visit was a mixed blessing for Robert, for the King was much taken by the place and no doubt there was a risk in not giving your Sovereign that which he desired. Robert handed it to the King and in exchange was given Bishops Hatfield, twenty miles north of London. Originally the Palace of the Bishops of Ely, Hatfield was later taken for the Crown by Henry VIII, who kept his children there, Mary, Elizabeth and Edward. The greater part of Elizabeth's childhood was spent in the Palace, and she was sitting under an oak tree in the park when riders from London arrived to tell her that her sister had died and she was Queen. The next day, with Sir William Cecil, later Lord Burghley, at her side, she held her first Council of State in the Great Hall of the Palace.

To have been given this old-fashioned place built in the late fifteenth century instead of his childhood home with its modern house and fashionable gardens must, to Robert, have seemed a very poor exchange. He set to, forthwith, to pull two-thirds of the Old Palace down and build a new house. Constructed in the shape of an E as a compliment to the old Queen, the house was a Renaissance palace, hung with gilded leather, velvets, silks and embroideries, and as rich in tapestry, silver, furniture and pictures as money and the modes and fashions of the day could make it. Outside, the house was enclosed by courts. There were the North and South Courts, a Great Court and a Little Court and within their walls were other buildings. We read of 'the castles at the coming in of the courtyard'. Each of these

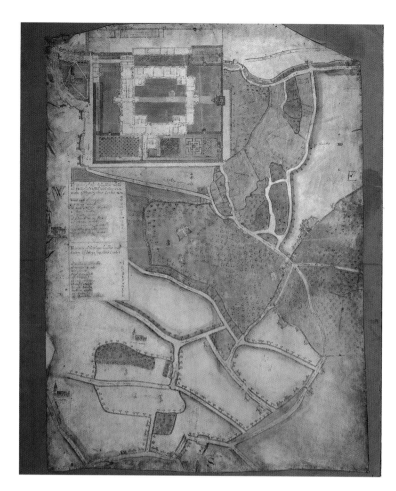

Plan of the Old Palace
gardens, about 1608

buildings was essential to the life of a great house. One held doves, one falcons, another hounds. There were the laundries, the smithy, a plumery where lead was worked for the windows, a house where ducks and geese were plucked to stuff the mattresses and pillows, a hound house, even for a short time a fox house. It was a world of its own, intimate and self-sufficient. Within the South Court, a pair of porter's lodges guarded the southern entrance gates, with their stone gate piers crowned by stone spheres.

Out beyond these courts were the gardens. Robert Cecil was a keen gardener, as were many of his contemporaries, notably his cousin Francis Bacon, who lived near by and was, later in 1625, to write a famous essay, 'On Gardens'.

Certainly Robert spared no trouble, pains or expense to design and plant a garden which would be a fit match for his new house. He had found, surrounding the old royal palace, elaborate gardens (we can get an idea of what these were like from some plans found in the archives at Hatfield) and he may have incorporated part of these into the designs for the new gardens, though they were to be far grander than what had gone before. It seems likely that Cecil's ideas might have been influenced by the contacts he had with Italy, for his friend Sir Henry Wotton was England's Ambassador to Venice at that time.

The making of the gardens was, at least in its early stages, supervised by Mountain Jennings, the gardener Cecil brought with him from Theobalds. In autumn 1609, he presented to Cecil the first plans, which he had drawn up together with a London merchant and garden expert named Robert Bell and a certain 'Bartholomew the gardener'. A paper in the Hatfield archives records how, in Bell's words, 'Wee did determine of a plott to bee drawne, shewed unto my lord, which I thinke will doe very well, and after may be chaunged or alltred at my lord's pleasure.' And Cecil did alter them, almost immediately, bringing in one of the foremost garden designers of the day, Salomon de Caus, a Huguenot engineer-architect from Normandy, to rework them. Sadly, none of the de Caus plans for the gardens have ever been found, despite exhaustive searches, but there are in the archives at Hatfield some descriptions by a Frenchman, a Monsieur de Sorbière, who visited the gardens in 1663, and it seems probable that they had not been much changed since Robert's death in 1612.

The French visitor appears to have been greatly impressed by what he saw. 'Hatfield', he writes, 'is a very fine castle – it stands very advantageously from which you have a prospect of nothing but woods and meadows, hills and dales, which are very agreeable objects that present themselves to us at all sorts of distances. Our nobility, and those of a more inferior degree, would have made use of the waters here, for some excellent uses and inventions, and more especially for a small river which, as it were, forms the compartments of a large parterre, and rises and secretly loses itself in a hundred places and whose banks are lined or boarded . . . when you come through the chief avenue to the parkside, and when the gates of the Lower Courts are open, there are walks present themselves to your view, that reach to the further end of the Park and make you lose your sight . . . we dined in a Hall that looked into a Green Plot with

two fountains in it, and having espaliers on the sides, but a ballister before it on which are flower pots and statues. From the parterre there is a way down by two pairs of stairs of about twelve or fifteen steps to another, and from the second to the third. From this terrace you get a prospect of the great Water Parterre that forms a fourth. There is a meadow beyond it, where the deer range up and down abutting upon a hill, whose top ends in a wood, and then bounds the horizon to us. There are also arbours or summer houses, like Turkish kiosks, upon some of the eminences, which have a gallery round and are erected in the most beautiful places in order to the enjoying of the diversified prospects of this most charming country.'

The steps leading from the courts and terraces about the house were lined with gilded and painted lions and led to the parterre where fountains played. From here you had a prospect of the Great Water Parterre designed by de Caus and described by de Sorbière above. 'You have also,' he writes, 'in those places where the river enters into and comes out of the parterre, open sorts of boxes, with seats round, where you may see a vast number of fishes pass to and fro in the water, which is exceedingly clear and they seem to come in shoals to enjoy all the pleasures of the place.'

Here, too, was a great marble fountain carved by the Dutch tomb carver Garret Johnson, the elaborate centrepiece with a great artificial rock in its basin on which stood a metal statue painted to resemble copper. The bottoms of the streams were lined with coloured pebbles and sea shells, and little leaden leaves, snakes and fishes were scattered about the face of the rock and the bottom of the stream.

The planting of the garden was entrusted to John Tradescant the Elder, and it was a mighty enterprise. In 1611, Tradescant was dispatched by Robert Cecil to Holland, Flanders and France, and other parts beyond the seas, to bring back rare plants, trees, bulbs and tubers, seed and flowers for the gardens at Hatfield. His bills in the archives also list for that date a chest of shells, with eight boxes of shells: these last were for lining the bottoms of the Water Parterre and fountains at Hatfield, and we read in the papers

Left Robert Cecil, first Earl of Salisbury, painted by John de Critz the Elder, about 1606–1608
Right William Cecil, second Earl of Salisbury, aged 35, painted by George Geldorp, 1626

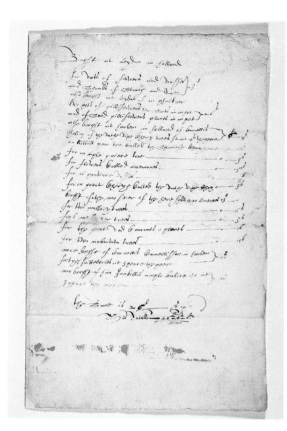

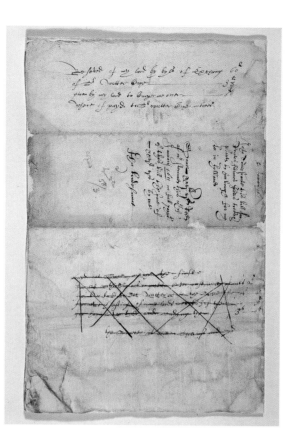

Tradescant's bill, dated 5 January 1612, for plants brought from Holland

of 1611 that 'in the East Garden the terrace walk is levelled and perfected, and the little river is indented and stones and shells laid in the bottom and to this day the water runneth in it'. That he laboured hard and long to make the gardens of his master at Hatfield the most horticulturally famous in England there can be no doubt. John Parkinson, whose herbal *Paradisi in sole paradisus terrestris* was published in 1629, called Tradescant 'a worthy, diligent and painefull observer and preserver both of plants and all natures varieties'. There is a seventeenth-century book, now in the Bodleian Library at Oxford, called *Tradescant's Orchard,* with paintings of fruit by Alexander Marshall. There is now some doubt about whether this is, as used to be thought, an actual record of the fruits Tradescant grew at Hatfield, but at the very least it provides a useful guide to what he may well have had there. There are peaches, mulberries, quinces, currants, apricots (Tradescant brought back apricots from North Africa when he went on an expedition there against the Barbary pirates), apples, plums, pomegranates and cherries, including the famous black heart cherry, with a special flavour, and the great nut.

We may imagine the scene in the gardens as they were being created. All is activity and work. Masons are building brick walls, banqueting houses, garden houses and fountains designed by Salomon de Caus, plumbers are laying pipes and trying to raise water to flow through the water parterre. Gardeners are digging holes to plant the trees, and making an end of laying all the grass knots, setting all the borders with pinks, Cecil's favourite flower, mowing the walks and grass knots, casting up brick dust and bringing it in, now raking, treading and beating the walks, watering the trees, dressing the pinks, weeding the walks and the quarters for planting. The carpenters are making doors for all the garden walls, four pretty straight arbours for the West Garden (which may have been the precursors of the four straight lime arbours that are there now, planted in a square) and finally working stools for the gardeners – we hope to give them an occasional well-earned rest, but more likely to stand upon to reach high branches for pruning. We know there was a mount in the West Garden because there is a note in the papers that the plumber had laid the pipes to it, and there is a description of four mounts made to overlook the bowling green in the East Garden, south of the first parterre garden, with the little garden houses by them.

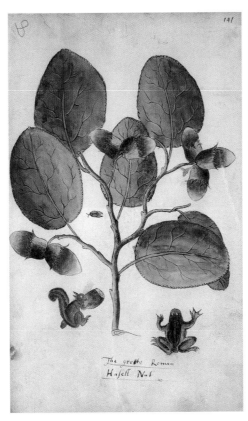 

Paintings from
Tradescant's Orchard
Left 'The grete Roman
Hasell Nut'
Right 'The harte Cherry'

Two banqueting houses were erected, and as we read of them, we immediately visualize a troop of serving men bearing dishes of victuals and sweetmeats for feasts on warm evenings or days of sun. Such delights could be enjoyed too in the elaborate garden houses with niches and pilasters being built in the same garden. There was also, near the Privy Garden, and looking down on the Royal Palace, an octagonal high pavilion; the outlines of its foundations still remain in the grass there.

We stretch our imaginations to the limit to try and visualize how the gardens looked, and it is painful to think of those lost plans, but to be able to have even an insubstantial vision in our mind's eye of how a garden of Hatfield's grandeur might have looked in the early seventeenth century, we must know not only something about the walls and buildings within it but which plants were growing there. Happily, our curiosity is largely satisfied by being able to read Tradescant's bills in the archives, and we know from them what a very large number and range of species he bought for the gardens. In January of 1611 he went to France, and spent £61.14s. on peach, pear, cherry and fig trees, Muscat vines, mulberries, a pot of double white stock gilly flowers (possibly *Hesperis matronalis* 'Alba Plena', which had been introduced at the end of the sixteenth century), a basket of shrubs, one pomegranate tree, six oleanders and eight pots of one-year-old oranges. He may well have been ignorant of the tender nature of these last groups of plants. On the same expedition, he went to Brussels and Holland where he bought a medlar tree, 50 walnut trees, some vines from the 'Archduke's gardener', double hepatica, white martagon lilies, *Iris susiana* and, notably, 1300 tulips for 10s. a hundred. The tulip may have arrived in Europe as early as 1554, the bulbs being sent there (he claims) by Ogier Ghiselin de Busbecq, who was the Austrian envoy to the court of Suleyman the Magnificent in Constantinople. The famous gardener Charles L'Écluse, or Clusius, may also have been one of the first people to have them. Clusius is thought to have been responsible for introducing many plants, including anemones, ranunculus, irises, narcissus, fritillaries and lilies, into gardens in Europe. One unique anemone was to become a cult. This was the great double anemone, *anemone pluchée*, also called the plush or velvet anemone – it had many names – and the first place it grew in England was at Hatfield.

The double or velvet anemone, as depicted in a flower painting by Jean-Baptiste Monnoyer (1636–99) at Hatfield

It seems not unlikely that Tradescant bought those 1300 tulips and this anemone from Clusius' garden at Leiden or from the Imperial Botanical Garden in Vienna, where Clusius had been before he moved to Leiden. Caccini, an Italian botanist and plantsman and a notable dealer in fine plants, had been growing the velvet anemone and it had evidently attracted much attention. This particular anemone was thought to be extinct but a few years ago was rediscovered in the South of France. How exciting it would be to grow it once again. The descriptions of its colours, of which there seem to have been great variety, are mouth-watering, and the paintings, tapestries and embroideries of the time in which this wonderful flower so often features make you understand the reason for the romantic aura that seemed to surround it. What a challenge for a plant breeder of today!

We do not know exactly when John Tradescant was born, but it was probably in the 1570s. At that time, the flowers grown in the gardens of Englishmen were of the simplest kinds. Violets and primroses, cowslips and marigolds, campions, lavender and rosemary and some flowers and plants brought in from the wild, not only for their beauty but also for their usefulness in medicine or in the kitchen. Every household had its garden of herbs, however grand or humble; the more sophisticated might include a few, very few, 'outlandish flowers' (as Parkinson called them) which had been brought from overseas. But, by the time Tradescant died, in1638, what a change had come about! Plants had been introduced in great variety and numbers and the gardens of the humble and the great had been transformed beyond recognition. This revolution in Western European gardens was a long-term consequence of the capture of Constantinople by the Turks in 1453 and the fear generated by the Turkish menace, which resulted in the European powers sending ambassadors to Constantinople. The envoys were enthralled by the Turkish gardens filled with exotic blooms, many of which came from Asia. As Dr Stearn says, 'never before or since has there been such an astonishing influx of colourful, strange plants into European gardens as when, in the second half of the 16th century, importations of unpromising onion-like bulbs and knobbly tubers from Constantinople brought forth tulips, crown imperials, irises, hyacinths, turban ranunculus, narcissus, lilies and anemones.'

Two other rarities that Tradescant brought back with him were the Catalonian jasmine (*Jasminum grandiflorum*) and the great rose daffodil, which still grow both at Hatfield and at Cranborne, the other Cecil family home in Dorset, whose garden was also planted by him. I like to think that the plants that flower in the gardens today may be the descendants of the very ones the great man introduced.

There are many roses listed in the bills for Salisbury House, in London, some of which must surely have found their way to Hatfield. The ones named 'great white roses' are most likely to have been Albas. Alhough there may be no certainty about their origins, some varieties, and perhaps their original forms, existed in medieval Europe. 'Murray roses' are more difficult and we may never be able to identify them, but 'parti-coloured roses' must, almost certainly, have been that rose of legend *Rosa gallica* 'Versicolor' or Rosa Mundi. It was a 'sport', a natural mutation, from *R. g.* var. *officinalis*, the apothecary's rose, used in medicine for its supposed properties. Another rose that could have fitted the bill for parti-coloured roses is the York and Lancaster rose, *R. × damascena* var. *versicolor*: sometimes the flowers are mottled blush-pink and white; more rarely flowers of different colours appear in the same cluster.

Portrait of John Tradescant the Elder, about 1630

Growing still at Hatfield are some ancient specimens of *Platanus orientalis*, one of the most magnificent of trees, long-lived and stately, with a wide-spreading head of branches and curiously dappled and flaking bark. Its bristly fruits hang like baubles from its branches. Originating in south-east Europe, it has been cultivated in England since the early sixteenth century and is known to attain a great age. Could Tradescant have planted these? It is possible. In the second edition of John Gerard's *Herball*, it is noted that there are 'one or two young plants' growing with Mr Tradescant.

Doubtless Tradescant would also have bought the mulberry trees that, according to tradition, were planted by James I at the four corners of the West Parterre. At the time, the King was trying to establish a silk industry in England but unfortunately he chose the wrong species: the King planted *Morus nigra*, the black mulberry, but the white mulberry, *M. alba*, is the one preferred by the silkworm. It seems unlikely that this would have worried Cecil; he had other matters to occupy his attention, and, anyway, the trees provided excellent fruit for pies, jellies and jams – as the only one of the four alive today still does.

But to return to the purchases Tradescant made in England and abroad. There is a bill dated April 1612 for seeds, and other necessaries for the kitchen garden. He bought onion, spinach, bugloss, borage and sweet marjoram, besides shears, rakes and mattocks. It is not difficult to imagine, as we read these lists, the energetic preparation for the spring work in the gardens. Still further purchases were 24 earthen pans for covering melons, two water tubs for them, and a scythe to mow the Courts and East Garden. Here gooseberries, raspberries, strawberries, roses and other flowers had been planted in what must have been a delicious *mélange*. Three and a half centuries later, George Eliot describes such a garden as her ideal, 'a garden full of homely plants, vegetables and fruit, a charming paradisiacal mingling of all that was pleasant to the eyes and good for food – you gathered a moss rose, and a bunch of currants the next; you were in a delicious fluctuation between the scent of jasmine and the juice of gooseberries, the

crimson of a carnation was carried out in the lurking of the neighbouring strawberry beds' (though in Tradescant's time the rose would have been an Alba or Damask, and the carnation probably a pink).

Monsieur de Sorbière further comments in the account he gives of his 1663 visit to Hatfield, 'I ought not to forget the vineyard, nor the several small buildings on the side of it, some of which serve as a retreat for several sorts of birds, which are very tame', and we should not forget it either, for it was a remarkable creation of Robert Cecil's: two great enclosures facing each other across the river Lea. To the south a steep bank falls down in terraces to the edge of the water. Elaborate walks enclosed by clipped yew hedges zigzagged down the slope ending in low banks of yew, and here the visitor steps on to a brilliant green sward sweeping to the borders of the river. Along the edge, yews were planted, no doubt in Cecil's day small clipped cones or pyramids, but now grown into immense trees with some of their branches trailing in the water. Duck, swans and other water birds still busy themselves on the river, as they have over the centuries.

Across the river to the north and enclosed by high brick walls is the garden where the vines were planted, 30,000 of them, sent by Madame de la Broderie, the wife of the French Ambassador to England. It faces full south and would seem to be ideal for producing grapes, but it has proved to be a frost pocket. This probably accounts for there being no record in the archives of wine having been made at Hatfield. Indeed the vines seem never to have been mentioned again, except by the fourth Marchioness, who said she remembered one of Robert Cecil's vines still growing in the vineyard before the Second World War; but there was little or no labour to care for the place during the war, and by 1945 there was no trace of the vine.

Now we come to a sad entry in one of the papers at Hatfield: a charge for mowing of the Courts and the East Garden against the funeral, for this was 1612 and Robert Cecil had died. He was only forty-nine.

It is a poignant thought that Robert had so little time to enjoy the treasures and beauty of the house he had created in only four years, or to walk amongst the pinks in the gardens he had planned with such loving care. Robert Cecil was a little man, less than five foot high, frail in physique with a hump on his back; he had been trained in statecraft by his father Lord Burghley to succeed him as First Secretary to the Queen. Low in stature he may have been, but he was undoubtedly great in intellect. As the French

The South Front of Hatfield
House. Print by T. Sadler, 1700

might put it '*L'intelligence même*'. Subtle, with vision, taste and imagination, he spent what time he could away from the affairs and cares of state and court, amongst the treasures of the new palace he had created, and the beauties of its garden. No detail of its making was too small for him; he supervised them all.

Robert Cecil's death in 1612 brought many things to an end and led to many changes. However, the new Earl, William, had an interest in maintaining the gardens, if not in innovation. John Tradescant continued to work at Hatfield until 1614. We have his bill of charges for 22 September 1613 to 8 February 1614. He bought items to encourage the growing of the melons, musk melons they were, 'namely two dozen of great glasses to cover them' (and melons were still being grown in glazed frames at Hatfield in 1665). He also bought a peck of rath ripe pease, onion and radish seed, 60 fruit trees for the Hatfield garden, and nails for tying the trees in the gardens of Salisbury House in London.

There are few records after 1615 to tell us what changes there were, if any, in the gardens during the next fifty years, but there is evidence that they were well cared for. In his diary for 1643 Evelyn makes mention of the gardens and vineyard at Hatfield. 'Went to see my Lord of Salisbury's Palace at Hatfield where the most considerable rarity besides the house were the garden and vineyard, rarely well watered and planted.' He praised the 'labyrinth and little mount, named the Mount of Venus'. 'It is upon the whole', he said, 'one of the most beautiful spots in the world.' Pepys, visiting Hatfield in the summer of 1661, though describing the second Earl as 'my foolish Lord Salisbury' and noting that 'the rain was coming through the roof of his house', was full of praise for the place, 'the chappel with brave pictures and above all the gardens, such as I never saw in all my life, nor so good flowers, nor so great gooseberries as big as nutmegs.' And there is also, of course, M. de Sorbière's record of 1663.

However, after William's death, in 1668, the gardens began to decay. Of the next five earls, Lady Gwendolen Cecil, one of the third Marquess's daughters, has written: 'the general mediocrity of intelligence the family displayed was only varied by instances of quite exceptional stupidity.' As far as can be discovered in the archives at Hatfield, none of them took any interest in the gardens.

The sixth Earl was something of a black sheep, shocking society by marrying his steward's niece,

Print of Hatfield House from the south-east by W. Watts, 1783

abandoning her and their children and going to live with a mistress at Quickswood, an Elizabethan house belonging to the Cecil family near Baldock. His chief delight was to drive the stage coach to London and to consort with pot-boys in the local inns. He sold many of the beautiful things bought for Hatfield by Robert Cecil – the early inventories make painful reading. And he seems to have done nothing to maintain or improve the gardens, which mouldered and slept.

The caprices of garden design could be compared with the modes and fashions for clothing the human body, though perhaps moving at a rather slower rate. By the time of the seventh Earl, and first Marquess (he was given a marquessate by the Prime Minister, Pitt, in 1789), the landscape movement had arrived, not without much controversy along the way, concerning the relation of art and nature. In gardens, art and nature are linked together and are meant to harmonize: if art plays a more prominent part, we arrive at formality in design, but if nature is left to her own whims, we get nearer to a freer or 'landscape' form of design. With this new movement, we arrived at a situation where the garden had little to do with the house, when before the house played an integral part in the design of the garden. The distinction (it has been pointed out) is evident: up to the eighteenth century, the object of garden architecture was to lose nature in art, not to lose any evidence of art in the presentation of nature.

The paintings of Claude and Poussin influenced the garden artists, who translated what they observed in these canvases into the picture painted, as they saw it, by nature; lakes appeared in the middle distance; instead of avenues, trees were set in 'clumps'; lines were serpentine, never straight – Hogarth defined serpentine lines as the 'lines of beauty, suggestive of vastness, sublimity, infinity'; and, to use another observation of the time, 'a rotund uniformity of curved forms' could, if the scene demanded it, be brought into view in the shape of a temple or obelisk.

Inevitably, the new style became exaggerated and suffered at the hands of parodists, much as the old style had. We remember Bacon's scathing opinion of knots, written in his 1625 essay 'On Gardens': 'in the main garden which should be square, under the windows of the house, there should be no fussy decoration, none of the knots, or figures of coloured earths' which, he says, 'are but toys; you may see as

good sights many times in tarts.' Later, Pope satirized the craze for topiary which arrived with the Dutch when William of Orange became king. He mocks and ridicules the fashion in a catalogue he produced, advertising such delights as 'St George in box; his arm scarce long enough, but will be in a condition to stick the dragon by next April' and 'Adam and Eve in yew; Adam a little shattered by the fall of the tree of knowledge in the great storm. Eve and the Serpent very flourishing.'

Now Hogarth was accused of trying to prove that the line of beauty lies in an 'S'. 'All our professors of horticulture seem to have the most idolatrous veneration for that crooked letter at the tail of the alphabet. Their land, their water must be serpentine, and because the formality of the last age ran too much into right lines and parallels, a spirit of opposition carries the present universally into curves and mazes.' The question was gravely discussed 'whether a modern gardener would choose to go to Heaven by any path that was not serpentine'. 'To lay out an English garden, one only has to get one's gardener drunk and follow him about,' a French wit commented. Another critic expressed the hope that he might die before the leading exponent of the landscape movement, 'Capability' Brown, arrived in Heaven, as he would insist on making the most of its capabilities.

Despite the critics, the movement swept the country. Country houses were stripped of their enclosed courts, their squares and their knots, their arbours and formal canals and walks. The surroundings of the Palace at Hatfield did not escape the fashionable destruction. The gardens, already in a state of decay and probably collapse, were largely swept away and the park, in the prevailing fashion of the day, was brought up to the walls of the house. A paper at Hatfield admiringly refers to what to us seems disastrous vandalism: 'His Lordship', it reads, 'has . . . with much taste and judgement, removed the walls with which the House was heretofore surrounded, an improvement which has enabled us to give a view of this celebrated place.' The seventh Earl, soon to be the first Marquess, even pulled down all the small buildings within the courts, including the beautiful gatehouse which was the entrance to the court on the north side of the house. One of the illustrations in *Dr. Syntax* gives us a glimpse of the gatehouse with the first Marchioness riding by.

'A noble hunting party', illustration by Thomas Rowlandson for *Dr. Syntax*, 1821

The interests of the first Marchioness of Salisbury were in gambling and hunting, not in plants and gardening. She was a wild Irish girl, Lady Emily Hill, daughter of an Anglo-Irish peer, Lord Downshire; though not as famous as the Duchess of Devonshire, her Whig rival, and without Georgiana's celebrated charm, she was nevertheless a considerable character and Creevy, while calling her 'Old Sally', described her as the 'head and ornament and patroness of the beaumonde of London for the last 40 years'. She hunted up to the day of her death, strapped to her horse and nearly blind, with a groom who told her when they got to a fence, 'Jump, damn you, Milady!'

Her son had different tastes. With the accession of the second Marquess, in 1823, Hatfield was, probably for the first time since the death of Robert Cecil, in the care of an active and interested gardener. He restored the gardens round the house as he thought they had been when they were first created in Jacobean days. He made terraces on the east and west sides of the house, unfortunately higher and wider than the original ones, thus spoiling the proportions of those aspects. He laid out new parterres and a maze, the plan of which was given to him by his friend Lord Mahon, whose maze at Chevening Lord Salisbury had admired on a visit there. The brick openwork walls that surround some of the gardens were built by him and he rebuilt the four garden houses at the corners of the South Court which had probably been removed by the seventh Earl. The brickwork was carried out with mid-nineteenth-century bricks, large and of a mauvish hue. To our eyes, all the second Marquess did had a very Victorian aspect and 'feel'. Many of the alterations to the gardens were inspired by a visit to Hatfield by the young Queen Victoria in 1846: indeed, the finishing touches to a great set of gates in the South Court were being made as the Queen's carriage came round the corner of the house.

After the death of the second Marquess in 1868, a Mr Bennett ruled as Head Gardener and he seems to have been a very creative one. We only have to read the *Gardeners' Chronicle* of May 1874 to see just how industrious and inventive he was. He planted a pinetum filled with trees from North America, spruces, firs, sequoias, which are still there along with an araucaria and a cryptomeria; a Garden of Perfumes; a new Kitchen Garden; a Rosery Garden before the Old Palace. All that as well as redesigning Robert Cecil's garden on the east of the house, repuddling the lake, and creating a rootery and a shrubbery. The *Chronicle* waxes quite lyrical about Mr Bennett and his achievements, describing how he moved old glasshouses from the Melon Ground and erected them to join the many new ones. 'Mr Bennett has a quick eye for the merits of what is old as well as new in horticulture, and has what young men of less ability and experience would call a weakness for old houses.' There were strawberry, peach, fig, vine, cherry, camellia and young vegetable houses, not to speak of houses growing pelargoniums, calceolarias, pansies, violas, and innumerable other plants used for the carpet bedding which filled the elaborately patterned formal parterres.

To follow Mr Bennett's creations, inventions (heating the greenhouse from heat generated from lime kilns) and building activities, two great conservatories constructed in the Pinetum (now the Wilderness Garden), and one along the foot of the East Terrace, let alone his horticultural achievements, leaves the reader quite breathless. Mercifully, he was not a destroyer of the few remaining features of the earlier gardens, leaving, for instance, the four mulberry trees planted by James I in the West Garden.

I well remember the Rootery when I first came to Hatfield in 1945. It was to the south of the New Pond (still called that though created by Robert Cecil in 1607). It was difficult to believe it could ever have been charming. Mud paths wound between hummocks of bare earth crowned by dark evergreens. Little light, and certainly no sun, penetrated the gloom. Romantic it was not: bats or vampires you could expect, but not the nightingale. My parents-in-law, the fifth Marquess and Marchioness, disliked it thoroughly, and replaced it with grass and bulbs and I, in 1988, when relining the pond and relandscaping the area around it, swept the last gloomy vestiges away.

The fifth Marquess and his wife were both enthusiastic gardeners, knowledge-able, and what would now be called 'hands on'. When his father, the fourth Marquess, died he was still deeply involved in politics and much in London. None the less, his greatest pleasure – and his wife's – was to plan and plant the garden at Hatfield, as

View of the East Garden by 'E.P.', 1851

well as to work in it when time allowed. Although the Second World War was not long over, and labour was in short supply, they achieved much in the gardens. One of the fifth Marquess's favourite leisure occupations was to clear the over- and undergrowth which, after four years of neglect, was rampant, and to feed the bonfires he made. He designed the eight square box-edged beds which you see now in the East Garden, while in the Wilderness Garden and on the east side of the New Pond, the two of them planted many azaleas, rhododendrons and camellias, though not a great number of these thrived, as well as large numbers of ornamental trees and shrubs.

In 1972, the fifth Marquess died, and my husband, the sixth Marquess, and I came to live at Hatfield, while remaining part of the year at Cranborne, the family's other seat in East Dorset, where I had been working on the garden for thirty-three years. I knew the gardens of Hatfield well, having first seen them in 1945, and had often idly wondered how they could be improved. It was rather different to realize they were now my responsibility to run and perhaps to redesign and develop – a daunting thought but a challenging one, too.

I knew at once what seemed to be absolutely wrong about the immediate surroundings of the house. The great house that Robert built still stands, much as he built it, save for some details. Then there had been more colour, with painted sundials on the towers on the southern sides. The coat of arms over the entrance was probably painted and gilded, and the finials of spheres and metal flags with 'R.S.' cut in them on the roofs of the towers were gilded too. The house must have had a richer look. None the less, the building was much as Robert's eyes had seen it in 1611, a Jacobean palace marvellously unchanged. Not so the gardens. Elizabethan and Stuart gardens, although in many ways homely and simple, were architectural too, and in a subtle way adhered to strict rules of form. They were, as we have already seen, very much extensions of the house they surrounded, and with it formed a blended whole most comfortable to the eye. This must have been very true of Hatfield: the walls of the courts were close to the house, much closer than they are now. The house when I first saw it was divorced from its gardens ,and its surroundings had been much changed, to something that seemed altogether alien to it.

My first thought was to try to replace, as far as possible, the intimacy between the house and its gardens. At the same time I had to accept that without the mind, feelings and outlook of those gardeners of long ago, and with so much irrevocably altered, it would be quite impossible aesthetically or financially to attempt to replicate physically what they had created. However, I have learnt all that it has been possible to learn about the original garden made by Robert Cecil and his son, as well as something of Tradescant's and de Caus' work there, and my ideas, plans and plantings at Hatfield in the last years have been profoundly influenced by this knowledge. Starting with Tradescant's lists of plants and trees, the descriptions of the gardens in the seventeenth century and everything I was able to glean from papers and bills in the archives, I went on to read all the literature I could on the gardens and plants of the period and to visit other gardens of this time, in England and abroad. Gradually, a picture formed in my mind's eye of the gardens as they may have looked in the seventeenth century.

I felt, as the Elizabethans and Stuarts did, that I did not want to break with the past. They, simply, by following their principles of beauty and sense of form, tried to make lovelier all that was most attractive in medieval times. I looked at how Jacobean gardens had developed from the earlier gardens of Classical and Roman times, through those in Renaissance Italy, whose gardens had widely influenced the designers in France, from where these new ideas crept slowly over to England.

Bacon's ideal garden was created, in his imagining, much in the Italian manner, while for his garden and palace at Hampton Court Henry VIII employed an Italian architect, John of Padua, and many Italian craftsmen. Hatfield also was much influenced by the Italian taste. The English Ambassador to Venice, Sir Henry Wotton, was a friend of Robert Cecil's. It seems more than probable that new ideas of the ordering of gardens could have reached the great man's ear through his Italian contacts.

Nearly four hundred years later, the Italian influence showed itself once again. This is how it came about. My greatest problem had been to decide where to begin the restoration of the gardens. The canvas was so huge. Mercifully, the problem was decided for me by the absolute priority of restoring the Muniment Room, where precious archives and books were kept. This does not sound as though it had much to do with the gardens, but the room had been built in the nineteenth century and was letting in damp, had no environmental controls, and had become quite unfit for its purpose. During the war years nothing could be done about this, and the books and archives had been brought into the house where they were obviously vulnerable to fire and water.

It took the best part of three years to restore the Muniment Room. The East Terrace was dug up, the rooms underneath made waterproof and the terrace reinstated. During this process, to our great excitement, we discovered the line of the original Jacobean terrace. Faced by the same bricks as the house, it was, as we had suspected, much narrower and three feet lower than the one built in the nineteenth century. It was enormously tempting to reinstate the original, which would have restored the proper proportions of the house, but this was a dream that could not be fulfilled and a compromise had to be reached. The dreaded gravel which surrounded the whole house was removed from the terrace and grass and paving laid instead, and a low wall in Jacobean proportioned bricks topped with Portland stone took the place of the Victorian openwork wall on the terrace's eastern edge. The very ugly nineteenth-century garden staircase had to be taken down to allow work on the Muniment Room, and it was at this point that the Italian influence came into play. The terrace looked down on a series of descending terraces, much as many Italian gardens do. Why not build a perron in stone, of two descending staircases to the right and left with stone balustrading? We had seen similar designs in Italy and returned to look at them and others. The decision to go ahead with the perron was made on our return. Meanwhile, we remembered we had found in Italy, many years earlier, four seventeenth-century stone statues, which had come from a villa near Lake Como. When these were taken out of store they appeared to be entirely sympathetic to the design and the right size and proportions, with all the figures looking outward as though surveying a distant view. But could they be relied on once placed on the pillars of the balustrade still to look in proportion? It seemed unwise to fix them without trying them, but how to pose these high and heavy creatures without the great danger of their toppling over and crashing below? They were too heavy to be held. Even our intrepid stonemasons, never before stumped for an answer, could not think of a way. Then I had an idea. Ask four of the smallest men on the Estate to come and pose, drape them in dustsheets and hey presto! There was the answer. The proportions seemed to be good, a photograph was taken and there were smiles, not to say laughs, all round.

Once the terrace had been laid with turf and paving, attention could be given to its planting. There were already several good plants against the walls of the house, including a rose 'Albéric Barbier' and a *Magnolia grandiflora*, which had, in the past, always been severely pruned and had never flowered. I allowed it to grow away from the wall, and this has encouraged it to flower abundantly. A deciduous magnolia, *M. denudata*, the yulan tree, was also there, one of four of this beautiful tree, planted against the walls of the house in the late nineteenth century. I added a *Paulownia fargesii* whose buds, if they escape frost (as they are formed by September) come into flower in May. I had read somewhere that a paulownia should always be planted where it could be looked down on. Here was the perfect position to see if this was right and it was. In the weeks of May, from the windows of the State Drawing Room, you can look down on a veritable surging sea of cream and heliotrope-purple scented flowers.

The Italian influence continued with the planting in 1977 of two walks running east and west framed by holm oaks (*Quercus ilex*), their heads, on seven-foot stems, clipped into spheres. My first idea had been to have them as a square *allée*, but I realized that as all else was square in the garden, a contrast of form was needed, and they must be round. They came from a nursery near Florence.

The holm oaks instantly provided a frame for the garden, now known as the East Parterre, where the fifth Marquess had removed the old patterned beds of box, gravel and polyanthus roses (at one time called Lord Burghley's Parterre) and made sixteen large square box-edged beds. In these I planted flowers and shrubs for all the seasons. In the spring they are filled with primroses and polyanthus, narcissus, early tulips, hepaticas, hellebores and euphorbias. Later, early irises, forget-me-nots, double wallflowers, May tulips and Scotch roses appear. There is also one notable plant from the fifth Marquess' time, *Paeonia suffruticosa* 'Rock's Variety' (now called *P. rockii*), given to him by Sir Frederick Stern of Highdown fame, which stuns with the beauty of its huge white flowers with maroon-blotched centres against its dark leaves. For full summer, I planted many old-fashioned roses, lilies, peonies, irises, carnations and pinks, cistus, violas and pansies, and a plethora of English roses with their scented old-rose-like flowers and repeat flowering. For late summer and early autumn, there are old-fashioned small-flowered Michaelmas daisies looking like the mists of the season. In the centre of the beds are large box topiaries with concave sides facing the four corners, creating a more orderly structure to the plantings and a background for them. A guest remarked that they look like mitred bishops embracing their flock.

Wide paths made of a coarse kind of hoggin in a nasty gingery colour surrounded the whole garden and were exceedingly uncomfortable to the feet. The gravel was removed and was largely replaced by paving, with cobbled patterns here and there.

I lined the walks beneath the holm oaks with fine Breedon Amber gravel which, if well tamped and rolled down, is almost weed-proof and is not picked up by the feet. Under the trees and in the gravel, I planted *Iris danfordiae*, a deliciously scented little yellow iris. Planted in the gravel the bulbs do not break up after flowering, never to flower again, as they do when planted in earth, and now they flower every year. I also planted *Oxalis enneaphylla*, which loved the gravel but appreciated the shade less. The borders under the walls on the east, north and south, which had previously held annuals, were all widened and planted with old roses, herbaceous peonies and tree peonies, and many other plants and bulbs for every season of the year. I had nowhere to plant the special small treasures that, if planted in borders, would be overwhelmed and disappear, never to be found again. Two corners that had been covered over with the horrid gravel gave the answer. Dug up and prepared with a good gritty mixture of soil and then a layer of fine grit to the depth of a couple of inches, they were ready for the species crocus, tulips and cyclamens, blue corydalis, baby irises and other precious alpines; the one corner in light shadow, the other in full sun.

My husband, who had a good eye for the architecture of a garden, had seen that the steps that led to the next terraces were too wide. This fault was disguised by planting yews (*Taxus baccata*), which grew into rounded columns, marching from just beyond the Italian wall fountain under the perron towards the far steps. At the same time, two of the square beds in front of the perron were halved diagonally to open up the space, and four stone early-eighteenth-century statues from the same villa in Italy were placed, two on either side of the steps to the second terrace and two facing each other north to south in the central grass walk.

There was still one important lack. There was nowhere to sit, to rest and look at what I hoped was going to be worth looking at. Stone bench seats seemed to be the answer and one more visit to the Italian stonemasons produced these. They are set in box (*Buxus sempervirens*) topiaried into comfortable embracing shapes to keep out the wind. I learned a tip from that inspired gardener Le Vicomte de Noailles, who put cork mats on his stone garden seats at the Villa Noailles to protect one from getting a damp bottom.

The photographs in the second part of the book will take the route most often followed by visitors to Hatfield, who come in by the entrance gates on the north side, and proceed to the West Gardens. However, having begun the description of our developments and alterations on the eastern side of the house – where they did, indeed, begin – I shall continue there, taking in next the Maze, the second terrace, the Pool Garden and the New Pond, then the Cascade and the Gainsborough Pools, which composed one of my three swan songs just before I left Hatfield after my husband's death. I will then return up the hill to the Kitchen Garden, Orchard and Mount Garden before considering the South Courts and moving from there to the West Gardens.

The gigantic maze is on the third terrace. It is of yew and often mistakenly thought by visitors to be as old as or older than the house, though it was only planted in 1841. Because it had been neglected during the war years and after, it had fallen into a near disastrous state of disorder and decay and it took fifteen years to get it into shape. I remember it being cut with sickle and stick, when it took many weeks to finish. Now, kept in shape by the extraordinary skill of Larry Laird with an electric hedge-trimmer, it has the precise lines of an architectural drawing and its annual trim is completed within three weeks.

The walk above the Maze was again gravel, as were the very wide paths running down either side. These were grassed down and the lavender hedge outlining the upper walk had to go too as the lavender looked peculiar against the grass. Instead, I planted tall box hedges with enclosures either end housing Lutyens oak seats found elsewhere on the estate. Eight huge stone urns, brought from Malta in the nineteenth century, were moved here from the outer South Court and planted with pyramidal Portugal laurels (*Prunus lusitanica* 'Myrtifolia'). Never far from my mind were the lists of plants Tradescant had used and his way of mingling flowers with fruit and even vegetables. There was a space between the box hedge and the retaining wall of the second terrace. I decided that sixteenth- and seventeenth-century plums, pears and apples, interspersed with the occasional climbing rose, should be fan-trained against the wall: one of the plums was grown at Fotheringay and romantically linked with Mary Queen of Scots during her imprisonment there. I had a vision of apple trees with their heads of clotted blossom being visible from the windows of the house in spring so I planted them (grafted on free-growing stock) between the wall and the hedge and underplanted them with gold-laced polyanthus, which are happy in the light shade and moisture afforded by the trees. This polyanthus was a florists' flower and though it was little esteemed by the ordinary gardener, perhaps because of its sombre hue, during the nineteenth century it attained cult status amongst the weavers and spinners of Yorkshire and Lancashire where, for successful exhibition, their flowers had to be circular with sharp gold edges and round, clear centres. I think mine would win few prizes but I find them utterly charming whatever their shape and centres look like.

Below the box walk, a bank encloses a lawn used for croquet with, at either end, a large mulberry tree (*Morus nigra*) planted by the fifth Marquess. Now, when the fruit is ripe, sheets are spread out under the trees, which are given a good shake, and the fallen fruit is used to make pies, jams, jellies and a particularly delicious ice cream. This area I left unchanged.

To reach the next terrace, you walk down an avenue of apple trees. These I planted to run down on both sides of the Maze. They are made up of old varieties, some very old and probably grown in Tradescant's time. I underplanted them with varieties of *Crocus chrysanthus* in blues and creams for the spring when the trees are in blossom, and with oxeye daisies for when the trees are hung with fruit. A grass path to your left leads on to what was the gravel path of a raised walk and is now lined with apple trees which look down on a long rectangular pool. This was a swimming pool, coloured a 'Californian' blue and lying below a grass bank. It looked somehow brash and out of place. Moreover, the yew hedges were uncomfortably low with big gaps, so winds from every quarter could buffet and freeze the unfortunate bathers. The first thing was to fill the gaps and let the hedges grow high, encouraging the yew to form arches over all the entrances. In addition, having placed two Lutyens oak seats, one at either end of the pool, I planted curved yew hedges behind them, for greater shelter, and to give a more comfortable feel to the sitter than they might get from an open 'doorway' behind their back.

Cydonia oblonga, the common quince, was introduced to England by the Romans, and since John Tradescant brought it to Hatfield in 1611 it has been planted there in every century. It shows especially well when planted as a standard, with its large white rose-tinted flowers and scented golden fruit looking like something from a medieval tapestry. I planted four, two at either end of the pool, and in the centre of the crescent-shaped space on its eastern side a *Gleditsia triacanthos* 'Sunburst' given to me by a generous friend. The quinces are underplanted with *Limnanthes douglasii*, a fragrant hardy annual which is singularly labour-saving as it renews itself each year.

I saw this garden as a green space, quiet and peaceful, with the only flowers the apple and quince blossom and the only colour a touch of gold. And so it has come about. The Californian blue has vanished and on each of the four corners of the now tranquil-coloured pool stand Italian stone lemon pots planted with rosemary. The twelve-foot-high hedges are braced at intervals with clipped buttresses, while a beautifully carved stone statue by the sculptor Hamish Horsley surveys the scene from the centre of the yew hedge on the raised walk.

Hatfield House and the New Pond, by F.W. Hulme, about 1847

Of course, as soon as the sun comes out, the tranquillity vanishes and the space echoes to the cries of happy bathers; but rarely are English summers warm for long, and the pool garden soon returns to its normal atmosphere of dreamy peace, occasionally interrupted by chubby little call ducks visiting from the New Pond.

There were many changes and much work to be done outside the formal gardens. The New Pond, possibly the site, or part of the site, of the Great Water Parterre designed in Robert Cecil's time by Salomon de Caus, was losing water through 'swallow' holes in its lining. The fourth Marquess, when he relined the pond, had employed a man and his son who came from Dorset and were the last people who knew how to make dew ponds, those mysterious 'scoops' on the Dorset downs that watered the animals grazing there. Father and son set to work, lined the pond with chalk from a nearby quarry and turned a herd of cattle into it. They fed them with straw, which throughout the winter they trampled into the chalk, making an impenetrable lining.

We could only line it with blue clay, which we did, and hope for the best, our skilled adviser, Keith Wesley, warning us that there would always be the occasional swallow hole, which there has been – something to do with water finding its own level which I'm not sure I fully understand. A sadness was the loss of the two noble beech trees that were growing on the island, at least two hundred years old. When we relined the pond, water must have been trapped in their roots and in spite of boring down to drain them, they died. While the New Pond was empty, we discovered a rather interesting thing. There was strong evidence that it must have been relined about every fifty years. The whole area looked like a building site with this vast hole in the middle.

The relining of the Pond gave us the perfect chance to do a little gentle landscaping round it. This was done and the last vestiges of the grim Rootery were bulldozed away. But it was not until the hurricane winds in the autumn of 1989 and the January of 1990, when thirty-nine and then fifty-six major trees were lost in the gardens alone, that the wood on the rising ground above the eastern side of the Pond could be cleared. The major trees felled by the wind there included an ancient *Zelkova carpinifolia*, a majestic tree at least two hundred years old. The tragedy was that its roots were not severed, they bent as though made of rubber, and if it had not been of so great a height that no machine could pull it up, it could have been saved. It took two years to clear the garden of the aftermath of these storms, with the result that where before it was impossible to penetrate the thickets of thorns, nettles and brambles, the wood, which has come to be called Pond Wood, is now, with its grassed woodland walk and young trees planted amongst the few remaining giants such as the two huge plane trees (*Platanus × hispanica*) introduced by Tradescant, and some fine beeches, a place of delight. Good has really come out of evil. In the last years, I have spent many a happy hour there, planting cyclamens, wood anemones, hepaticas, dog's-tooth violets, snowflakes and snowdrops. Already there were carpets of *Narcissus pseudonarcissus*, the first few bulbs of which were brought from Hart's Copse at Cranborne, where they grew as a native wild thing, by Lady Gwendolen Cecil in the early 1900s. Before the storms, there were a few poor strangled bluebells struggling for light; now they have seeded and spread in the dappled sun and freedom of the cleared woodland.

To create the New Pond, Robert Cecil had built a dam. Its northern side drops precipitously down, into what is known as the Dell. This name has not changed in four hundred years – it is frequently mentioned in the archives in papers dated 1610–12, notably one of 1611 from a Thomas Wilson to the Earl, describing how 'the Frenchman [almost certainly Salomon de Caus] means to make a force at the going out of the water from the island which but the current of the water shall drive up water to the top of the bank above the Dell and so descend into two fountains.' It is exciting and perhaps not too fanciful to think that this grand design has, though in a much more modest way, been reinterpreted in the Cascade and Pools I designed four hundred years later for the same site. Many snowdrops grow there and I made a mown grass path running down from below the Kitchen Garden on the west to lead into it, planting many ornamental and forest trees on the way, adding to my collection of oaks, now numbering over a hundred, and planting myrobalan plums, with their clouds of white blossom sometimes as early as March, acers and a variety of white-trunked birches. When the snowdrops are over, they are divided and now they spread widely up the steep sides of the dam's bank and further into the woodland and Dell.

Many years ago, a large terracotta overflow pipe had been inserted into the wall of the dam, emerging on the other side. After heavy rains when the Pond was over-full, the water crashed down into the Dell and was lost in a ditch below. What a waste. Whenever I came to the Dell, my vision transformed the ugly pipe into a rocky hole with a rush of water cascading down the hill into a series of pools below. The years passed and my dream remained unfulfilled, with much other priority work to be done.

Then, in 2002, two things happened. I went to the Gainsborough exhibition at Tate Britain and saw there a small landscape of a waterfall cascading down into a succession of pools below and thence into a lake. I was transfixed. The landscape depicted a scene almost (minus the lake) exactly as I had imagined it for the Dell. I contacted my friend Karen Hearn at the Tate and she kindly sent me a photograph of the picture. The second thing that happened was the discovery, on consulting our Head Gardener, Mr Beaumont, whose philosophy is 'anything can be done' and whose enthusiasm and energy for any new project is boundless, that he could find time to create the cascade. Picture in hand, we surveyed the site. Everything seemed to be possible and by 2004 the main elements were in place. Three pools, 12, 24 and 36 feet in diameter, were dug and lined with blue clay. They sloped slightly to the north and there were low weirs laid with slabs of stone which carried the water from pool to pool. There was a fourth circle, 48 feet wide, where a 5-foot canal of water surrounded grass in whose centre grew a *Quercus ilex* planted by the fifth Marchioness and now a shapely 50 feet high. It was, to an inch, exactly in the centre of the cascade. The northern boundary fence was moved back and Tamworth pigs introduced to clear the ground of nettles, brambles and bracken and to manure it. And then it rained. It rained and rained, on and off, for weeks, and all our plans for the final cultivation of the site and the sowing of the grass seed before the winter set in had to be reluctantly postponed until the spring of 2005.

One of the major changes in the gardens was the abandonment of a twelve-acre kitchen garden created in the late nineteenth century and the making of a new one to the north east of the house. To visit the old one, to pick a strawberry or pea or fetch a plant from the greenhouse, meant getting into a car and driving nearly half a mile. A time and motion study showed that we could lose seventy hours of working time in a week if there was bad weather and the gardeners had to walk that half-mile to work in the shelter of the greenhouse or potting shed. This did the trick and I was allowed to make the new kitchen garden. It faces full south with a brick wall on that side and tall whitethorn hedges on the other three. Whitethorn (*Crataegus laevigata* syn. *C. oxycantha*), which is studded with white scented flowers in May, was much used for hedges in the gardens of the sixteenth and seventeenth centuries. Because the ground slopes, the garden is on various levels, retained by brick walls and with steps for access. I made arched tunnels, with apples trained over them, leading to a small octagonal fountain surrounded by low clipped box. The stone figure in the centre of the fountain came from Italy and is of a naked child holding a fish, water flowing from the fish's mouth. There are arches with fruiting vines, and morello cherries were planted against the north wall and a potting shed and greenhouse erected. A narrow raised border where alpine strawberries are sometimes planted is the only place I know where you can pick them without getting backache.

With the move from the old kitchen garden, where there was a famous 'pear ground' (the Hatfield pears swept the board at the London fruit shows) and much other fruit, thought had to be given to where an orchard could be made. Luckily there was a spare piece of ground, an area entered from the Box Walk through a low seventeenth-century wrought-iron gate which I had found in France in the 1980s. Enclosed by high beech hedges planted by the fifth Marchioness, it seemed to have no particular purpose and I thought it might admirably suit the planting of a small orchard. So it was roughly divided into squares by mown paths and planted with apples, pears, gage plums and cherries, mostly on dwarfing stock for ease of labour. This last was a mistake as the trees are more prone to disease on dwarf stock, something which we did not know at the time, and in 2003 they had all to be removed and replaced by half-standards.

In the orchard grass, I planted a wild flower mixture given to me by Miriam Rothschild. Sadly, only the knapweed seems to be happy there; the other beauties did not flourish and have vanished. I experimented with bulbs of *Narcissus* 'Hawera', to see if it would tolerate the thick grass. Happily it does and has spread with its pale yellow flowers, two or three to a stem, showing well in May, when the grass is not too high. I planted *Crocus chrysanthus* too, and a great many cowslips, and for late show *Camassia quamash* (syn. *C. esculenta*) with its sapphire-blue flowers. Here in the orchard we placed the beehives. Mr Beaumont, amongst his many other talents, is a skilled beekeeper and there were several years of successful honey crops before the dreaded varroa mite arrived from Asia and wiped out all the colonies.

There was an outer orchard to the south, also surrounded by beech hedges, where there were some old apple and damson trees but little else and I planted a small area of it with Kentish cobnuts, the nuts usually being stolen by the dastardly grey squirrels who always knew they were ripe before we did.

I come now to the last garden on the eastern side of the house, known as the Mount Garden. It is described in the archives as having four mounts surrounding a bowling green. Two of the mounts have disappeared but there is one left, and half another, with a huge horse chestnut tree growing on it. Both were in a bad way, with their shape largely lost. Returfed and reshaped, one at least would, I hoped, become like the mount described in an Elizabethan paper I had read, 'a little hill to be scrambled up to view a fair prospect'. The prospect from the top of the greater mount is of the East Terrace, the East Parterre and the Great Court, or Outer Court, on the south of the house, and one day perhaps a wonderful design Alec Cobbe did for us of a 'kind of Turkish kiosk' will be built and placed there and you will be able to view that fair prospect. You will remember Monsieur de Sorbière's description of 'the hills with kinds of Turkish kiosks on them'. I asked a friend who lived in Constantinople if she could find out what Turkish kiosks of the seventeenth century looked like. This she gallantly did, and the result was Alec Cobbe's drawing.

I made some other small alterations and additions to this garden. A pair of *Prunus avium* 'Plena' was planted, one on either side of the entrance to the Orchard through the beech hedge, and a wide flower and shrub border removed from below the eastern wall of the outer South Court, and the space grassed down. We planted *Arbutus menziesii* 'Marina' along the length of the wall. Tender when young though hardy later, they had a harsh first winter and may not survive. On either side of the steps leading from the East Terrace, I made a small area of well-drained gritty soil for small treasures, where they would have the protection of the terrace walls. A honeysuckle and pale pink wisteria grow there, a rare climbing rose, 'Docteur Rouges', and a flourishing *Myrtus communis*, grown in the sixteenth century and covered in white flowers in July and August.

In 1998, the work of removing the gravel from the South Court and West Terrace was begun. This, for me, was a significant and defining moment. My prime objective had always been to re-create, if at all possible, the intimacy between the house and its garden, which seemed, as far as my researches could discover, to have properly existed between the two when they were first made in 1611. The plan was to replace the gravel, and some York paving which the fifth Marquess had laid in the Inner Court some years earlier, by grass and Purbeck stone setts. Would this achieve the effect that we hoped for? That was the great question. The first thing was to do some more research. The stone quarries in the Isle of Purbeck in Dorset were contacted and Mr Hayson of St Aldhelm's Quarry came to see us. He looked at the stone outside and inside the house and found that the steps to the doors in the Inner South Court were of Purbeck, as well as the footings of the supposedly Inigo Jones arcade. There were also paving stones of Purbeck in the basement of the house and Mr Harcourt Williams, our Librarian, discovered in the archives a mention of a Purbeck stone path in the North Court.

It was logical that Robert Cecil should have used Purbeck stone. His manor house at Cranborne in Dorset was not far from Purbeck, and this stone, which was brought to London by boat up the Thames, was much used in the courtyards of the city and also at the royal palace of Hampton Court. I went to look at the courtyard at Hampton Court to see how the stones were laid and noted the way they ran in the paths which led to various doorways and entrances in the courts. I was impressed by the harmony between the soft red brick of the walls and the parchment colour of the stone which had accumulated a certain amount of moss over the centuries.

Mr Edward Fawcett was someone who could divine not only water but the foundations of buildings too. I asked if he would come and see what he could find of the past in the South Court, and he discovered much that was extremely interesting. He found a complete parterre with beds outlined in stone, and banqueting houses on the east and west. His willow divining rod turned over very satisfactorily where there were the foundations of a wall, which must have divided the Inner and Outer Courts, and where there now grew a low yew hedge I had planted. He found too that the four garden houses were in their original positions. These were in a very poor state, most of them hardly safe to go into, as well as letting in damp and wet. They have now been put in order and, in 2004, their roofs were restored to their original shape, recorded in a dated drawing in the archives.

Next to be tackled was the redesigning of the Outer Court. I had always felt that the original level of the Court had been lower, with probably a stone ramp leading into the Inner Court – as is seen in a print of another Cecil house at Wimbledon – with the original height being on a level with the Park. This was proved to be so when the soil (which was largely rubble and stones) was removed, and the lower level was revealed to be topsoil. I would have much liked to have levelled the whole site but this was impossible because it would have to have led to the dismantling of too much. A compromise had to be reached. When the soil had been extracted, broad grass walks were left surrounding the areas at a lower level. The central path divided the two matching areas and led to the great cast-iron gates erected in the nineteenth century. The original gates, as we learnt from an eighteenth-century drawing, were wooden, and much lower than the later ones, with the pillars on either side crowned by stone spheres, and a delightful pair of porters' lodges guarding the entrance. When the soil came out, banks three feet high were left below the raised walks. I planted, close against these, box (*Buxus sempervirens* 'Suffruticosa'), to form a hedge to grow till it reached the height of the brick openwork walls, built by the second Marquess, which surrounded the site, so forming the raised walks which were typical features in gardens of the sixteenth and seventeenth centuries.

To fill the areas below the banks, I devised stylized patterns of clipped evergreens, four different designs surrounding simple circular fountains, their edges flush with the grass and their ten-foot-high jets falling into the water and so roughening its surface, making it difficult to see the golden koi carp which we introduced when Keith Wesley told me that they were kept in fish ponds and pools in the sixteenth and seventeenth centuries. I longed to do what Tsar Nicholas, the last Emperor of Russia, had done at Tsarskoe Selo, where the carp were tame and had little silver bells attached to them. When the Emperor and his family came to the fountains, there must have been a tinkling rush of sound as the fish swam up to be fed. What a delicious conceit and how the Elizabethans would have loved it! When the mutinous sailors from the ships at Yalta reached Tsarskoe Selo, they slaughtered the carp and stole their silver bells. Such a small barbaric act seems fittingly to signal the start of the seventy or so years of a great and bloody tyranny.

The four different designs for the clipped evergreens in the sunken areas of the Outer Court were a Tudor rose, oak leaves, a fleur-de-lys and a four-leaved shamrock. Oak leaves because they seemed to be typically of Hatfield, with its park and gardens full of ancient oak trees, including the oak under which Elizabeth was sitting when they rode down from London to tell her that she was Queen and the famous Lion oak, shown to Queen Victoria in 1846 as being of a remarkable size, which still has a splendid canopy of living branches from which, when it has a crop, acorns are collected and young 'Lions' grown on. Queen Elizabeth's oak, alas! now dead, though its trunk is preserved, was alive till the Second World War, and two trees, at least, grown from its acorns were planted near the site of the mother tree, by Queen Victoria and Prince Albert. They are both poor specimens, but occasionally produce a few acorns which have grown into useful trees. The shamrock symbolizes my Irish family and good fortune, and the fleur-de-lys marks the life in France of the third Marquess and our own. The Tudor rose needs no explanation.

My first idea was to plant evergreens in different tones of green, box, *Ilex crenata* and phillyrea, to be shaped and clipped in rounded forms, to look, I hoped, a little like veined green marble. The box, and to a lesser extent the phillyrea flourished, but the ilex was a disaster. It did not like the heat and the summer after it was planted was a particularly hot one, nor did it seem to like the soil; and in spite of feeding and watering, it did not thrive and had to be removed.

On either side of the central paved path leading to the great nineteenth-century cast-iron gate, I placed square artificial stone containers (by Blashfields of Stamford), each planted with a standard holm oak (*Quercus ilex*). They had been for many years standing empty in the middle of the arches in the arcade of the South Front. I had them moved to a position in front of the pillars of the arches and planted them with standard bays but they still did not look right and two plantings of bays were killed by frost. The Inner Court you might think the perfect place for more tender plants, being enclosed on three sides by the walls of the house and facing full south. I was quite taken in by the site but the bay trees taught me a sharp lesson. The cold air seems to drop into the Court and, finding no way to escape, blights the more sensitive plants.

These do better on the walls, and the *Magnolia denudata* growing by the window of the Chapel and facing east never has its flowers frosted. As a young bride, I was told that it was always out for Easter, no matter how early or late Easter was, and in my time it has been so. One year it looked dreadfully ill, and, very worried, we cosseted it like a sick child, giving it large quantities of liquid manure and a thick cover of rich compost. That did the trick. Its huge old trunk, from which most of the original branches had died, sprouted amazingly with vigorous new growth, which in ten years has nearly reached the roof.

I always feel a house should be enveloped with plants that look good all the year round, therefore largely evergreen and ever-grey, many preferably scented. The obvious ones, of course, are the homely rosemary and lavender, but there are several others, such as the sages, thymes and daphnes and *Choisya* 'Aztec Pearl'. In the borders round the house I planted some of these, interspersed by the occasional tree peony, dwarf flag iris and many roses. In the spring, there are bulbs, tulips and, for later in the season, lilies. One day, I had a fancy to do something completely different and decided to have only black and white plants and flowers around the house. Apart from some roses on the walls, nearly everything was already white. The black was more tricky but the search for it was fun and nearly completed in 2004 when I left Hatfield. Two more *Magnolia denudata* grow on the south walls of the wings between the towers and sometimes the first flowers are peering through my windows by the end of February.

To complete the sense of enclosure round the house, we planted yew hedges on the east and west, running from the corners of the East and West Towers of the wings to the corners of the garden houses. High wrought-iron gates in the yew completed this sense of enclosure.

We now walk through the west gates on to the terrace, once gravelled, but now with grass and paving in Purbeck stone. We go through another gate, another nineteenth-century cast-iron one but this time low, and into a walk planted either side with columnar hornbeams (*Carpinus betulus* 'Columnaris'). On our left lies the Wilderness Garden, which has too seen many changes over the centuries. The area covers 13 acres. Late in the eighteenth century it was called the 'Shrubbery', conjuring up not very attractive pictures in one's mind of dusty laurels and spotted aucubas surrounding suburban villas in nineteenth-century London. A note in the family papers of 1783 records the carting of gravel to the shrubberies at the cost of £52.10s. The gravel was still there when I first remember. A note dictated by the second Marquess reads, 'It is not known when or by whom the shrubbery was made or planted. The old Labyrinth planted in 1834 was removed to the east side of the house in 1840–41. Pinetum planted on the site of the old Labyrinth about 1843–44. Hot house removed and Ivy House taken down.' This is followed by the following, in brackets: 'I believe it was in the first instance planned by my Lord's mother.' This would have been the dashing first Marchioness.

In 1823, there is an inventory of the Shrubbery listing '6 flower stages, 1630 greenhouse pots and flowers, 2 square boarded bee houses and 7 stocks of bees in straw hives', which makes one think there must have been quite a considerable garden in the Shrubbery created by 'Dow Sal'.

The next time we read about it is in 1869, when 'A new conservatory was built in the Plantation of the S.W. corner of the house.' This my husband remembered well. It was 200 feet long and 20 feet wide, and in it was a Coade stone fountain. It was pulled down between the wars. The fountain was the only thing left, apart from the foundations of the great conservatory, when I came in 1945. There it was sitting in the grass looking rather forlorn.

One of the most interesting bits of information comes, in about 1900, from the then head gardener, Mr Norman, who said, 'The cypresses in the Shrubbery are of the same date as the house. A good many trees in the Shrubbery were planted about the same time, and close together, because the oaks have run up in a way they would not have done had they had proper room to grow.' How one longs to know what the trees he calls cypresses were! Would it be too extravagant to imagine that they could have been Italian cypresses given to Robert Cecil, or those trees' children? Cypresses grow easily from seed and live to a great age. Four, grown from seed I collected in Sicily, survived out of doors at Cranborne for years, and the Shrubbery is warm and sheltered. One thing I feel pretty sure about is that a magnificent giant of a sweet chestnut (*Castanea sativa*) growing there dated from the first Earl's time. I talk of it in the past because it was lost in 2001 when one of its mighty branches fell, bringing the whole tree down with it. We did everything we could to save it, pollarding it and pulling its great trunk upright. But it was summer and a time of great heat and in spite of soaking the roots and spraying its trunk and remaining few leaves, we lost it. I mourned that tree. It was a friend. Tradescant could have planted it. Sweet chestnuts can live for a thousand years. But, thank God, we have several of its children and they are flourishing.

The Pinetum was planted with the trees that typically were brought triumphantly back from the Americas and Canada by the plant-hunters of the time. These included redwoods (*Sequoiadendron giganteum*), various conifers such as *Abies cephalonica* and *A. pinsapo* and *Araucaria araucana*, the monkey puzzle, first introduced by Archibald Menzies in 1795 and later by William Lobb in 1844. It could have come to Hatfield at either of these dates. When it loses the leaves from its slim curved twigs, they make admirable lighters for candles (especially on the Christmas tree) as they contain a resin which when the tips are stuck in the fire give a little, long-lasting, blue flame. I fear they would not pass the current Health and Safety regulations.

When we did the new planting in what is now called the Wilderness we had to contend with not only the foundations of the old Conservatory, but those of the Hothouse and the Ivy House as well, not to speak of the concrete platforms where Nissen huts were built during the Second World War when the house was a military hospital. I believe some of the trees that we planted may not have grown well because their roots have come up against some of those remains.

Carrying on with my vendetta against the hoggin gravel, I grassed down the paths in the Wilderness and laid out a rough herringbone pattern of grass paths, with new-planted trees defining them, mowing roundabouts round the ancient trees (and some of the younger ones) that came in the centre of the paths.

The fifth Marquess and Marchioness had planted many rhododendrons and azaleas (as well as some kalmias, pernettias and pieris). The soil was not ideal for them and they did not thrive. I have removed some of the least happy ones and the rather violent purple, red and orange hybrids. Luckily the prettiest seem the happiest, especially the pale scented azaleas with flowers like honeysuckle and the great white scented rhododendron that flowers very late. *R. augustinii* is pretty too, and there is a group looking well at the top of the Wilderness when the bluebells are in flower. Here there is a spectacular carpet of them spread between the oaks and beeches and when the wood is sunlit, there drifts on the air a subtle scent of balsam. Gerard called it 'a strong sweet smell somewhat stuffing the head'. There are lily-of-the-valley too, growing under an immense cedar of Lebanon, the last of three that must have been planted in the eighteenth century. Not far away are groups of standard *Amelanchier canadensis*, the snowy mespilus, with its cloud of white blossom that, annoyingly, is over far too soon. Here and there amongst the forest trees, I planted *Prunus avium*, A. E. Housman's 'loveliest of trees'. I planted too, groups of birch, its chalk-white stems underplanted with snowdrops and hellebores; and on either side of one of the main grass paths is an informal avenue of *Acer japonicum*, all grown from a batch of unnamed seedlings. Young as they are, they already make their mark in the autumn when their leaves turn.

A *Davidia involucrata*, the pocket handkerchief tree, discovered in China by the French missionary David in 1869, was planted by the fifth Marchioness in the 1960s. It had never flowered. It is a greedy feeder, and I was told to pile on the manure every autumn, which I did. Still no flowers. So one day, walking in the Wilderness, I went up to it and told it that if it didn't flower the next year, I would cut it down. I know this is hard to believe but the following May it put forth one flower and each year since it produces more. I have planted many white camellias to join the pink ones planted by the fifth Marquess, which are now huge bushes. Eucryphias have flourished for late summer flowering and there are species roses for May. Sheets of *Crocus tommasinianus* and other crocuses flower in early spring, followed by primroses and cowslips grown from seed, which are spreading far and wide. Cuckoo-pint and wild orchids are beginning to appear, as, since 1972, the long grass, before then cut in June, is not cut until late July or early August, depending on the season, so the seeds of the bulbs and wild flowers have time to ripen and fall. The grass in most of the Wilderness is coarse and long, as in other areas of the gardens where it is not mown closely. To reduce its height and thickness, we have planted yellow rattle which is a parasite on the roots of grasses. We bought seed to start with, but then collected our own, and more and more areas of wild garden are sown with it. It is a pretty wild flower with yellow blossom, and is magical in its effect on coarse grass. Its parasitic ways create a much thinner cover on the ground, so allowing the wild flower seed to penetrate the earth more easily, and new wild flowers suddenly appear which till then have had too little light and air to allow their seeds to germinate.

Magnolias do well, and I planted quite a few. *Magnolia × loebneri* 'Merrill', *M. × soulangeana* – a group of seven – and *M. × s.* 'Alba', as well as *M. campbelli* subsp. *mollicomata*, for which you need to have patience, as it takes ten to fifteen years to flower. Why didn't I begin all my operations in the gardens by planting trees, hedges and screens to hide the boundary fences? It was foolish not to and I've regretted my stupidity ever since, especially when I contemplate little trees six to twelve feet high when I could be looking at giants thirty years old.

The hurricane winds of 1989 and 1990 devastated the Wilderness near the house. Mr Beaumont remembers being woken by the roar of the wind. Dressing to go and see if the greenhouse was all right, the force of the tempest was such that he could not get out of his front door to take a step forward. Heavy thuds and crashes marked the fall of forest giants. I heard the same depressing sounds, and the noise of the tornado was as though an express train was coming into the house.

What a mournful scene met us the next morning. The north end of the Wilderness had lost the greatest number of its ancient trees. After two years of clearing and making good the site, the replanting began. The new trees have not grown particularly well. There is no great depth of soil here and it is anyway rather stony and poor. Gravel over London clay, with an occasional patch of something better, plus rare outbreaks of chalk, is what we have in the 45 acres of garden, and we have to make the best of it, which is hard work, though things are easier in the flower gardens because we build up the fertility of the soil with organic fertilizers such as fish, blood and bone, calcified seaweed and large quantities of the homemade compost which has come to be known as the 'Hatfield Pudding'.

One of the trees I am particularly fond of in the Wilderness is a tsuga with four exquisite red-brown trunks crowned by a canopy of dark evergreen foliage. There is also a malus (*M. baccata*) which in spring with its large white scented flowers is a treat to look at and to smell. It was there in the Wilderness when I came and one year it decided to carry an immense crop of fruit and when the thick carpet of its little apples had deposited their seeds, a veritable forest of seedlings appeared. We grew many on. They grew at an immense speed, as trees can do when they are planted from seed, and in a very few years they graced many places in the wild parts of the garden.

When I walk through the garden in autumn, another malus, 'Comtesse de Paris', brought from France, reminds me of Yeats' lines:

> and walk among long dappled grass,
> and pluck till time and times are done
> the silver apples of the moon,
> the golden apples of the sun

On either side of the little avenue of columnar hornbeams that lead towards the Holly Walk, I have planted *Iris reticulata*. It was an experiment I gloomily thought was very likely to fail, but I deemed it worth a shot. The grass was thick there, perhaps too thick for them to succeed. But my gloom was misplaced. They have done well over five or six years and have even increased. Emboldened by this modest success, I planted the hybrid tulip 'Lilac Wonder' and some *Iris latifolia* which have done well too.

The planting of the Hornbeam Walk was the first part of what was to become the second of my Hatfield swan songs. It was to lead to a pair of stone steps which would take you, if you turned right, to the tall wrought-iron gates, standing between brick pillars with stone spheres on them, which lead into the Scented Garden. If you should turn to the left, you would find yourself in an avenue of *Malus* 'John Downie'. They have been there many years, and very lovely they are in the spring, with thick white blossom, and in the autumn with large red fruits, but I planned to do something new here. This was to complete the walk from the south-west Garden House down the hornbeam avenue, which framed it, into the Holly Walk. It was going to need rather careful planning and planting as I felt it must not look like a flower garden because it was fringing the Wilderness. I planted tall box plants to eventually form an archway over the pair of steps and another facing it across the path. Huge plants of box planned to be clipped into billowing forms lead on the right and left from the entrance gate to the malus avenue. A paved path forms a narrow border on your right, under the fifteenth-century brick wall of the Scented Garden. On your left, there are four large beds divided by short paved paths, the central one leading into another narrow avenue, this time of limes. More huge box bushes have been planted to form an informal hedge, likewise clipped in billowing fashion which I hoped would give a certain purposeful sense of enclosure and a more gradual transition from the planted beds into the wild. Again, purposefully, I planted these with woodland lilies, small-flowered species peonies and roses such as *Rosa* × *odorata*, some hostas, heucheras and a *Viburnum* f. *tomentosum*, and planned to plant some woodland bulbs as well as less sophisticated climbers on the wall. There are already many hellebores, and some *Fritillaria pallidiflora* which seem to be very happy.

At the end of this walk, another pair of stone steps takes you into the Holly Walk. This is a curious place which has seen a few changes since it was planted in the nineteenth century. It was first made by the third Marquess. He was then both Prime Minister and Foreign Secretary and found it difficult to get any exercise for his eighteeen-stone frame. The Walk was laid with asphalt and a holly hedge planted either side and it ran the full length of the 200-foot Conservatory to the wall of the Royal Palace Yard beyond. Here, as well as on narrow asphalt paths he had had laid all over the Park, the Prime Minister took his exercise, riding a tricycle. A boy perched on the back with his hands on the Prime Minister's shoulders, ready to jump off and open the gates for him.

By the 1970s, the asphalt was much decayed and full of weeds and was not a pretty sight. However, my husband had happy memories of roller skating on it with his brothers and viewed it with much sentiment, so it was a while before it was swept away and put down to grass. Several more years passed and then, in 2002, the moment came when it could be tackled. It needed a good deal of shaping up, as in some places it was one width and in some another, the hedges bulged forward or recessed back and the grass walk was not level. I visualized it as a quiet green space, a contrast to, and a retreat from, the flower gardens, their colour and their busy-ness and activity. It should, I thought, be strictly architectural. It was then that I remembered the Borromini Gallery in Perspective which I had seen many years ago in the Spada Palace in Rome. It was the wish of Cardinal Bernardino Spada, who delighted in Baroque virtuosities, and he asked the architect Borromini, who was already working on the restoration of the Palace, to design it. It was built in a year, in 1652, in collaboration with the Augustinian mathematician Giovanni Maria di Bitonto. The real measurement of the Gallery is 8.82 metres, but it has a virtual depth of 35 metres. The optical illusion is created by the convergence of the planes of the colonnade and the ground slope of the floor towards the vanishing point. Four or five years of growth will be needed to shape the pillars, their capitals and bases and the hedges themselves before the right effect is achieved in the Holly Walk. Fanciful? Yes, and not exactly a Gallery in Perspective, but inspired by one.

Borromini's Gallery in Perspective in the Spada Palace in Rome, built in 1652

The Walk is now edged with stone and at the south end is the vast head of Queen Elizabeth 1 in artificial stone. She had sat on the roof ever since being brought from the façade of the old Royal Exchange in London, which was rebuilt in 1825 after a fire. We had a plinth made for her, and now she broods in stately splendour not far from where she spent her girlhood. At the north end of the Walk, there is an Italian copy of an early-eighteenth-century limestone seat.

A high wrought-iron gate leads from the Holly Walk into the Scented Garden. This was the first flower garden that I redesigned, beginning it in the mid-seventies. If an integrated design was to be achieved here, much had to be altered. The royal palace had been on the main road from the North to London and almost certainly the broad path running from the great oak gate, with a postern in it, to the wrought-iron gate in the south in this garden was part of that road. There is a story which I was told by the fourth Marchioness that Henry VIII was riding south and his daughter Mary, a virtual prisoner in the Palace, heard he was coming, and rushed up the stairs to the Tower to look out of the window to try to catch his eye. He did not even look up. What a brute he must have been.

This road, or path, had the usual hoggin gravel on it, which, when removed, was replaced by the Breedon Amber and edged either side with York paving, the uneven edges facing into the centre. On one side was a broad border backed by a wall. This wall must have been the west wall of the Privy Garden –

which we know about from a plan of it in the archives – protecting it from the London road. Unfortunately, in the nineteenth century it was much reduced in height, but its lower half has the original Tudor bricks. The garden is enclosed by two other sixteenth-century walls on the north and south, and on the west by the hedge lining the Holly Walk; all of them had broad borders in front of them. The beautiful walls were largely hidden by huge shrubs and the border below the hedge was on a slope and came for no obvious reason well beyond the bottom step of the stone stairs leading to the Holly Walk. There was a great deal of bedding out and in the centre of the garden were two huge *Malus* 'John Downie' which looked very out of place. I took a deep breath and removed them. Then I pushed back the sloping east-facing border to the line of the steps, which meant it became a raised border faced by a retaining wall of brick. I had the two other borders divided in half lengthways by narrow York stone paths and subdivided from back to front by a broader middle path and two narrow ones. Now you could see the beautiful Tudor brick walls and see and smell the plants growing on them. *Azara serrata* and *Trachelospermum jasminoides* thrive on the north-facing wall, while *Cytisus battandieri* with its scent of pineapple and *Clematis rehderiana*, smelling like cowslips, grow with other scented wall plants on the one facing south. One of my favourite moments of the year is when the row of four half-standard plum trees 'Czar' blooms in the spring, with a cloud of scented white blossom. It is equally wonderful in early September when the rounded heads of the trees are hung with purple-blue fruit.

At the heart of this garden is the Herb Garden, enclosed by a hedge of clipped sweetbriar, *Rosa rubiginosa*, the eglantine of poetry and medieval tapestry and illustration. The scent from its foliage pervades the air, especially after a shower of rain or in humid weather. It has a delicious fruity smell, like ripe apples. Several of its hybrids are grown with it, including the double marbled sweetbriar, which is irresistibly charming. Paved paths lead to a sundial surrounded by a circle of chamomile, and with thyme planted at its foot. All the paths, paved at their edges, originally had chamomile planted in their centres but the feet of thousands of visitors were too much for it to bear and it had to be replaced by Breedon gravel.

The cook has a long but rather agreeable walk through the garden to where I have planted the herbs, a collection of everything that she might need for her soups and sauces, sweets and meats. The mints, which walk everywhere, have been planted in bottomless containers to control their wandering roots and eight standard honeysuckles (*Lonicera periclymenum* 'Belgica') grow near by. The main beds in the Herb Garden are edged with parsley, which rather unexpectedly grows like a low hedge, its colour a vivid emerald green, a colour unlike any other plant I know.

There are four pieces of lawn on either side of the Herb Garden, divided by paved edged paths. These have their centres planted with grass, and pass through high box hedges with *oeilles de boeuf* (peepholes) giving a view into the garden. The four paths lead you under clipped arches of box, into circular green bowers, the box rising over a frame. Four panels are open to the sky, four closed by box, but, as I write in late 2004, it will be four or five years before the bowers have grown enough to complete the vision I had of them in 1997: places of sun and shadow, of quiet contemplation, where you could sit on one of the four stone benches, write a poem and listen, as the simple jet drops water into the bowl below, and the box, on a sunny day, lightly pervades the air with its musky, dusky scent.

This is a garden crammed full of a thousand different scents. Scent of shrub and tree scents, springing from flower and foliage, bulb or tuber and not failing to produce them in every season. Even in the depths of winter there is sweet bay (*Sarcococca hookeriana* var. *humilis*), clipped as a low hedge and scenting the air for yards around in February, and the wintersweet (*Chimonanthus fragrans*) with its pale yellow waxy flowers marked with ox-blood red. Then in spring there are the plums and the intensely sweet flowers of silver-leaved *Elaeagnus commutata*, and the sweet-smelling tulips 'Prince of Orange' and 'Prince of Austria', auriculas and primroses, the sweet violet, and daphnes, of course. Then lilies, *Lilium regale* and *L. auratum*, lilies-of-the-valley and sweet geraniums, every one with a different scent – spice, peppermint or rose, or a scent uniquely its own. There are white Guernsey stocks grown from seed gathered in Guernsey itself and its purple sister known as the 'Guernsey Violet'; the white one I have planted like a hedge, either side of one of the paved entrance paths. The broad west-facing border I divided (either side of the main entrance into the Scented Garden from the Privy Garden), by making paths leading to seats, planted in their centres with many different scented thymes, which have a difficult time surviving the visitors' feet. In this border, as in many of the others, there are also old-fashioned roses, the Damasks, Gallicas and Centifolias, as well as scented roses for the walls, and the English roses, bred by David Austin, which look like the old ones and smell as sweet, but flower till the first frosts. A pair of standard quince trees on either side of the main entrance is hung in the autumn with deliciously scented golden fruit which remind me, rather nonsensically, of the nursery rhyme, 'I had a little nut tree and nothing would it bear, but a silver nutmeg and a golden pear', for golden pears are what they look like.

In the north-east corner of the garden, a flight of stone steps takes you into the Privy Garden. As you climb them, to your left, a bothy-cum-toolshed, forms, with the walls, a warm corner. The pretty rose 'Climbing Pompon de Paris' grows near the door and on the other side *Lonicera fragrantissima*, covered with sweetly scented cream flowers in late winter and spring. There was, on the right of the steps, when I first saw the garden, a horrid kind of rockery set with what I believe are called 'pudding stones', made of small pebbles stuck in lumps of cement. Not pretty and not improved by a planting of rather tired old yuccas. Removed as soon as possible, it was replaced by narrow terraces faced with brick, filled with gritty soil and chippings, and planted with scented alpines and bulbs and a wonderful-smelling *Muscari macranthum* with huge yellow and purple flowers. It came from Kew, and was given me by my friend Sir George Taylor, then the Director. Against one of the pillars of this entrance to the garden is a very old plant of lemon verbena (*Aloysia triphylla* syn. *Lippia citriodora*). It is tender and has to be wrapped up in several layers of bracken and sacking each winter, but in late May it leaps back into life again, its leaves making a delicious summer tisane. The top of the wall here is draped by *Clematis armandii*, with, in April and early May, huge tresses of creamy white flowers, lightly scented.

Someone said that fragrance was 'the voice of inanimate things', and it is certain that it can stir the memory and take us back to other moments in time: very rarely sad moments; sometimes glimpses of one's childhood, a certain smell recalling a much-loved home, the scent of lilies, tobacco plants and sweet rocket in the June warmth of a dusky garden brings back past loves, the scent of a malmaison carnation a beloved grandmother who always had one pinned to her bosom; the scent of a tuberose, a summer night in Venice. Everyone with a sense of smell will be moved not only by the immediate sensual pleasure of a delicious scent but also the memories and feelings it can evoke.

Above the Scented Garden lies the Privy Garden. A plan of this, dated 1608, exists in the archives, and in the 1900s Lady Gwendolen Cecil used ideas from its design when she created her parterre. She was clever in the imaginative way she planted the yew hedge surrounding this parterre: instead of a rigid square it has a graceful curve. At the centre of the parterre is a large fountain, planted with waterlilies and in it there are golden and silver koi carp. The fountain is not, sadly, one of those designed by Salomon de Caus, but the octagonal centre basin is very old and could be one of his.

There was a great deal of bedding done in this parterre, and there were many harsh-coloured modern roses. The soil was stony and poor and the patterns of the beds were somewhat lost. We dug and fed and replanted and at the same time allowed the hedge to increase in height to give more secrecy and shelter. The corners of the hedge at either side of each of the four entrances were allowed to grow enough to be clipped into finials and the four corners of the yew hedge to rise, forming snug enclosures with stone benches from Italy on platforms of brick, and a clipped yew sphere on the hedge behind them. Many new plants were introduced here and many of the labour-intensive bedding plants eliminated, although quite a number of old favourites have been kept. There is room for tall things here like sunflowers and hollyhocks, some of the taller David Austin roses, *Euphorbia characias* and *E. c.* subsp. *wulfenii*. I have tried to have colour and form here at each season and in early spring there are, amongst other things, clusters of *Iris reticulata*, as well as species tulips, *Euphorbia amygdaloides*, polyanthus, ipheion, sometimes called triteleia, and perennial wallflowers. These are followed by many tulips in early May with peonies, iris and the main flowering of the roses and lilies, to be followed, as summer fades, by the last of the roses, late lilies, Michaelmas daisies and alstroemerias.

Outside the yew hedge there are lawns and at each corner is a mulberry tree, one of them said to be the last of those supposedly planted by James I on his visit to the house. I have replanted the other three, and made octagonal wooden seats to go around them, and have propagated King James's tree. A walk surrounding this garden on four sides is covered by a canopy of pleached lime (*Tilia × europaea*), of unknown age, but thought to have been planted in the late eighteenth century. There are two arbours at each end of the western side of the walk above the Scented Garden, where there are two early-nineteenth-century groups of figures in artificial stone against the brick wall. They also came from the Royal Exchange: one is of Queen Elizabeth and her Court, with Sir Thomas Gresham and Lord Burghley amongst them, and the other is a group of classical figures of Britannia with emblems of Commerce and the Polite Arts. The walks under the limes – more of the third Marquess's paths for exercising on his tricycle – were covered in black asphalt. It was exceedingly ugly, cracked and weedy and the whole garden perked up when it was removed and the pretty Breedon Amber gravel was laid.

At the sides of the Lime Walk in spring there are sheets of violet and white crocus, *Anemone blanda, A. b.* 'White Beauty', and *A. appennina*, as well as *A. coronaria* and *A.* De Caen Group, double and single white-flowered forms. They are supposed to be tender but are happy in the grass and come up year after year, and an unknown white saxifrage has spread generously amongst them. Still in the Lime Walk, under the wall of the West Terrace, I have made a narrow border. Here there is broken shade, and cream, white and green hellebores grow sturdily with woodruff and white primroses, *Dodecatheon meadia* f. *album* (first introduced in the early eighteenth century) and a small-flowered white vinca, with white- flowered heucheras, a variegated Solomon's seal, snowdrops and a white *Puschkinia scilloides*. This small piece of the garden I find that rare and happy thing, almost entirely satisfactory. I say almost because only if the West Terrace were three feet lower would it be perfect.

Since the fifteenth century, several elaborate parterres have been designed for the Privy Garden. Some in their day were the height of fashion and much admired, and although to our eyes most of them appear very unsatisfactory, no doubt such taste will one day come back into fashion and attract many compliments.

One of the designs was described in the *Gardeners' Chronicle* of 1873. At that date, Mr Bennett, who we have already met, was the Head Gardener. He evidently did not think much of the Privy Garden's flower beds, which are described in the *Chronicle* as of 'odd design', and he replaced them with a basin of water with rockwork in the centre – 'the water dropping gracefully over it . . . Gravel walks of equal width strike traversely across the turf . . . the spaces between these walks are filled with twelve circular beds.' A year later, we read that 'these circular beds are admirably filled with pelargoniums and calceolarias'.

Here we leave Mr Bennett and his far-reaching designs and, walking out of the Lime Walk northwards and looking to the right, see a low nineteenth-century cast-iron gate which is the entrance from the North Court into the West Gardens. On your left as you enter, I made a raised bed faced with bricks. There is a tall yew tree growing here and two of the tallest and finest *Phillyrea angustifolia* trees I have ever seen. There are another two at the entrance to the East Gardens from the North Court. They must be nearly a hundred and fifty years old, with fine trunks and heads of evergreen foliage looking almost fashionably cloud-pruned. It is rare to see a tall phillyrea tree even in its countries of origin, North Africa and Southern Europe, but in sixteenth- and seventeenth-century England it was often used for hedges. Indeed, Evelyn recommended it as a hedge plant.

We are now in a quite large area of flat ground furnished with lawn and Breedon gravel paths, trees, statues and seats. There is an immense horse chestnut tree (*Aesculus hippocastanum*) with a wooden octagon seat around it. This chestnut is a native of the region between Greece and Albania and was introduced into England in the seventeenth century. It is a beautiful sight in May when it is covered with candles of white flowers. A walnut tree planted by the fifth Marchioness grows in front of the yew hedge looking south. You sit on the seat beside it and you have a view down the Lime Walk to the stone steps leading to the Hornbeam Walk. Another path to the east leads to a long wooden seat half-hidden by the box and yew clipped in a bower around it. All the paths are framed by box hedges. Now four and a half feet high, they are curved down, rising at each of the corners into shaped finials which are not yet fully grown but will, eventually, have small spheres on their tops. The main path leading to the chestnut tree has a row of standard medlar trees behind the box hedges that frame it. The medlars, a graceful umbrella shape, have large white flowers in the spring, and they are laden with fruit later in the year. You have to wait to pick the medlars till they have been 'bletted' by the first frost, otherwise they are not good to eat, but once 'bletted', though perhaps not to everyone's taste, they make an excellent pudding, puréed and eaten with cream, also a delicious jam or jelly.

Against the yew hedge facing west are four early-eighteenth-century stone statues which came from the same villa near Lake Como as those in the East Parterre. I have been letting the yew form niches around them which will give the eye something perpendicular to rest on against the rather monotonous horizontals of the rest of the hedge, and at the same time frame the statues.

This part of the West Garden lies above the garden of the Palace where Queen Elizabeth lived as a girl. So I thought to keep the planting here to trees grown at that period; a row of *Prunus rhexii*, a flowering and fruiting cherry planted by the Elizabethans, went in along the yew hedge which faced south, and very lovely they are in the spring. Mulberries were planted above the Knot Garden. These trees have an interesting history. In the 1990s, Hatfield and Villandry, the magnificent *château* in France with its famous gardens of much the same period, were 'twinned' one with t'other, and the Fruiterers' Company marked this historic event with the ceremonial planting of a gift of mulberry trees. A similar ceremony was carried out at Villandry, with speeches, a 'silver' spade and the officers of the Company planting the trees dressed in their fur-edged green robes. It somehow seemed a fitting ceremony for both Villandry and Hatfield. Both we and Dr Carvallo, the owner of Villandry, were not only honoured but entertained.

I had for several years much wanted to create a garden in front of the Old Palace and plant it with the flowers grown in the time of the Tudors, and those grown and collected by the Tradescants. In 1982, there was the opportunity to do so.

All that remained of the Old Palace was the Great Hall, with the Upper and Lower Solar rooms, plus a few rooms to the north. Robert Cecil had pulled down the other three sides of the Palace, leaving high banks framing what must have been the inner courtyard of the building. The fifth Marchioness had made here a simple garden of a border planted with old-fashioned roses, a central round pond, and four squarish areas of grass formed by paths paved in York stone. In each of the four grass spaces was a *Malus* 'John Downie', underplanted with *Scilla siberica*.

We can only guess what the area was like before the demolition of the three wings which had enclosed it, but most probably it was paved, though perhaps there could have been a simple garden for herbs. In the papers, there is an addition to the 'Notes of Hatfield House' dictated by the second Marquess in 1866–7: 'The Palace Garden was designed by my Lord, who just after he had given the design, found the ground plans of the Old Palace, and a garden of the same design.' We do not know if this note refers to the ground before the east front of the Palace or the area to the south where the Privy Garden lay. The first is the most probable, because in 1874 the *Gardeners' Chronicle* describes a garden called 'The Rosary' which was in the centre court of the Old Palace. It says, 'On the site of the palace of bishops and kings there is to be found a modern rosary, filled with the last new varieties, and planned with a cultural and constructive skill almost ahead of these emphatically go-ahead times . . . The rosary is almost hidden till the visitor approaches and looks down upon it: the effect is rich in the extreme. The Roses, from the sheltered position and the care bestowed upon their culture, have done well; the whole of their roots can be flooded from below, by means of a series of underground drains at pleasure. The rosary is a grand sight, its design is chaste and well suited for the plants, and its site, culture, growth and flowering are all as near perfection as could be wished.' 'Chaste' is such an eccentric adjective to use about a garden. One wonders which adjective gardeners of the twenty-first century might have used!

The first thing I had to do before designing a new garden for the Palace was to study the books in the library at Hatfield on gardens, gardening and plants of the period. Thomas Hill's *The Gardener's Labyrinth* of 1579 was one of them, William Lawson's *New Orchard and Garden* (1618) another, and there were others, such as Estienne's *Agriculture et Maison Rustique* (1594) with designs of knots. I looked at the knot garden at All Souls' College, Oxford, that at Jesus College and the one at Beauregard, near Blois, not to speak of knot designs on Celtic crosses, in stone carvings and on wood panelling (there are several examples at Hatfield), plus those in embroidery of the period, where patterns entwine in intricate circles as though sewn by the needle of Semiramis. There is even a knot in an embroidered binding worked by the eleven-year-old Princess Elizabeth on a book she gave as a present to Catherine Parr. Perhaps it was embroidered when she was at Hatfield.

Out of all this study and research came not only a greater knowledge of the history of gardening in the period, but the plans for the Knot Garden at Hatfield.

What exactly is a knot garden and how did it originate? Man's fancy for interlacing, interwoven patterns can be traced far back into antiquity, and knot designs developed over the centuries under the influences of war and peace, expanding trade, the venturing abroad of kings and emperors and a taste for chivalry and romance. In England the knot as a design reached its apogee in the ages of Henry VIII and Elizabeth; and so did the knot garden. With the rapid abandonment of defences under the secure rule of the Tudors and the development of the Tudor style, an elaborate formal layout for the garden evolved which was to be maintained for some two centuries. And although quite early in the fifteenth century the knotted bed had begun to take the place of the simple rectangle of previous years, knot gardens are largely associated in our minds with Tudor times.

Tudor knot gardens were beds laid out in formal elaborate patterns, the geometrical lines being planted with low clipped evergreens, such as germander, winter savory, santolina, thrift or box. There were closed knots, when the open spaces left by the interlacing, intertwining or geometric patterns of the closely clipped hedges were filled with flowers, or were entirely filled by the interweaving hedges; and open knots which, to give variety of tone, had the spaces filled with different-coloured earths, brick dust, or even ashes – or, according to Gervase Markham, flowers of one colour. In design as well as in intricacy, the Tudor knot exceeded all others, and if some of the ambitious plans which appear in contemporary gardening books were ever carried out, it must have exercised the skills and art of many gardeners to maintain them in their proper order.

Two events had a profound influence on the development and character of these gardens. One was the invasion of Naples by Charles VIII in 1494, nine years after Henry VII came to the throne. When the French took Naples, they were amazed by the gardens of Poggio Reale and La Duchesca and when they withdrew they took Italian craftsmen and designers with them. A host of new ideas invaded French garden design and from there spread northwards, and especially to England.

The second was the publication in Venice in 1499 of the *Hypnerotomachia Poliphili*. This story of a lover's search for his beloved takes the reader through a dreamland of architectural fantasies, classical ruins and gardens filled with elaborate topiary work, statues and flower beds, laid out in patterns which include the earliest known representations of garden knots. Colonna's dreamy vision of a Golden Age appealed to Elizabethan and Jacobean society, which delighted in symbolism, and was enthralled by tales of chivalry.

The knot garden also had practical advantages. First, it was an object of beauty and interest the whole year round: at its best perhaps in spring, it was almost as effective and doubly welcome in winter. Then, it could be applied to a garden of any size. Even the gardens of cottages could accommodate a knotted bed, often in the most intricate design. In larger gardens the space was subdivided into a number of symmetrical walled enclosures, separated by terraces or earth banks. From the eminence of these raised terraces the whorls and contortions of the knots could be seen and appreciated. Steps would descend from them to the parterres divided into halves and quarters by paths, and incorporating any diverse features, chief amongst them being the knot.

Among the best-documented gardens of the Tudor period were those of Hampton Court Palace. Expressing in their grandeur the magnificent panoply of Tudor riches, they must have made a profound impression on all who saw them. Cavendish, in a poem written in 1520 before Cardinal Wolsey handed Hampton Court over to Henry VIII, gives one of the earliest descriptions of its gardens:

> My garden sweet enclosed with walles strong
> Embanked with benches to sit and take my rest,
> The knots so enknotted it cannot be exprest,
> With arbours and alleys so pleasant and so dulce.

This verse clearly indicates the transition from the Middle Ages to Tudor times. The first couplet might be describing a medieval garden, the surrounding wall, the raised banks, the turf seats; in the second couplet we are in a sixteenth-century garden with its knots.

Some of the designs probably had symbolic meaning or had the monarch's arms and cyphers carried out in the plantings. Parkinson, whose *Paradisus* was published in 1629, discusses whether the garden should be orbicular, triangular or square, and decides on the last as being most practical. 'To form it therefore with walks,' he writes, 'cross the middle both ways and round about it; also with edges, with squares, knots and tails and any other work within the square parts.' Beds could be bordered with thrift but that had the disadvantage of sheltering snails 'and other small noisome worms'.

He goes on to discuss other plants for edging the knots, but dismisses them as having serious faults and comes down finally in favour of box, 'an edging of box, tho' it hath an ill scent' (I do not agree with him there!) 'is the best and surest herb to abide fair and green in all bitter storms of the sharpest winter and all the great heats', far preferable to germander, hyssop, slips of yew or juniper, or lavender cotton, which were difficult to keep in order.

And what of the flowers that were planted in the knots? In the fifteenth and sixteenth centuries, these were usually the English wild flowers with occasional rare plants brought by travellers from abroad, but as trade increased and travel widened, the 'outlandish flowers' began to arrive in ever-increasing numbers. Traders and plant-hunters brought tulips, the Catalonian jasmine, anemones, dianthus, oriental hyacinths, the ranunculus, columbine and Star of Bethlehem. Huguenot weavers, fleeing from the massacres of St Bartholomew, brought over a number of exotic plants that were ideally suited to the small enclosed beds – auriculas, pinks, primroses, violets, double daisies and thrift. Towards the end of the sixteenth century, the crown imperial, fair maids of Kent (*Ranunculus aconitifolius*), chequered daffodils (*Fritillaria meleagris*) and the tulip from Turkey had been introduced and by the beginning of the seventeenth century they could be found in every garden.

Spenser pictured the butterfly flitting amongst the herbs and sipping honey from the beds filled with the quiet simple plants of early Tudor days, and another poet, Michael Drayton, pictures vividly the flowers the Tudors would have looked at in their knot gardens:

> In anadems for whom they curiously dispose
> The red, the dainty white, the goodly damask rose . . .
> Then the odiferous pink that sends forth such a gale
> Of sweetness; yet in scents so various as in sorts.
> The purple violet then the pansy here supports . . .
> The double daisy, thrift, the button batchelor,
> Sweet William, sops-in-wine, the campion; and to these
> Sweet lavender they put with rosemary and bays . .

'Man', as Maeterlinck writes, had by the end of the sixteenth century and the beginning of the seventeenth, 'ventured forth from the cloister, the crypt, the town of brick and stone, the gloomy stronghold in which he had slept. He went down into the garden which became peopled with azure, purple and perfumes, and opened his eyes astounded, like a child escaping from the dreams of the night. His awakening was caused by the new treasures of blossom that met his gaze; flowers that must have

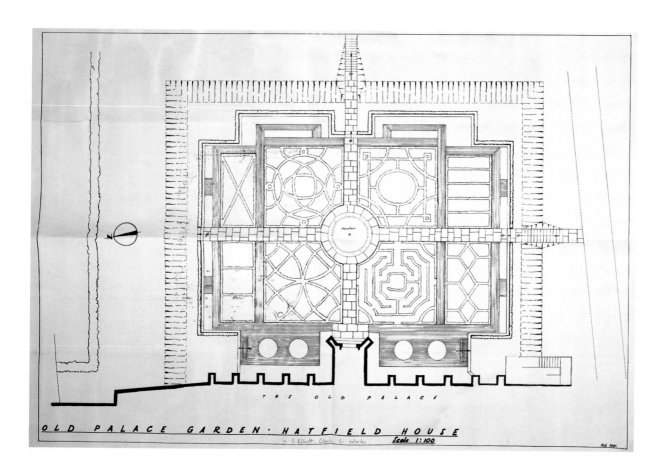

OLD PALACE GARDEN · HATFIELD HOUSE

Plan for the Knot Garden at Hatfield, designed by Lady Salisbury in 1981

seemed impossible to him, had been introduced as never before and the New World had begun to unfold its treasures.'

The Elizabethans loved symbolism, the strange, the bizarre and fanciful. They liked the striped and variegated, the double flowers, green flowers, the great rose plantain, hose-in-hose primroses, Jacks-in-the-Green, and this taste for oddities and the unusual was carried on into the seventeenth century. Here is William Lawson, whose work is typical of the most charming side of the Renaissance in England – of its delight in flowers and birds and all rare and beautiful thing in art and nature – writing in his *New Orchard and Garden* published in 1618 of 'the Rose red, Damask, Velvet, and double, double Province Rose; the sweet Musk Rose, double and single, the double and single white rose, the fair and sweet scenting woodbine, double and single and double double; purple cowslips and double cowslips and double double cowslips; primrose double and single. The violet nothing behind the rest for smelling sweetly. A thousand more will provoke your content, and all these by the skill of your gardener, so comely and orderly placed in your borders and squares and so intermingled that on looking thereon we cannot but wonder to see, what Nature corrected by Art can do.'

Nature corrected by Art – that surely is the perfect description of a knot garden and the formal, clipped, topiaried gardens of Tudor and Stuart England.

In the 1530s when Henry VIII's gardens were being planted, elaborately patterned knots had all the interest and excitement of a new idea, but already in 1613 they were beginning to pass out of fashion in the greatest gardens. Markham, in his *English Husbandman*, states that the knot 'which is most ancient, is at this day of most use among the vulgar, tho' least respected with great ones.' But patterns for knots continue to appear in garden books well into the seventeenth century, and even later, when the gardens of the nobility were being converted first to the French style as laid down at Versailles and Malmaison and then to the Dutch style favoured by William and Mary, the cottager's garden remained much as it had been in early Tudor times.

In the nineteenth century, following the decline of the landscape movement, there was a revival of interest in knot gardening, although the knot gardens of this time were far from being a true reconstruction of earlier gardens. They were very much of their era, Victorian or Edwardian ideas of what Tudor or Jacobean gardens looked like.

Today there seems to be a revival of interest in formal gardening. It is beginning once more to be admired, having always had a few faithful adherents. One of the possible reasons for this revival of interest is that in spite of a shortage of labour it has become possible to maintain such gardens. Clipping needs to be done only once a year, there is a machine to do it with and, as we have seen, knots can be made in any size to suit gardens both great and small. Another possible reason is that there seems to be a certain nostalgia for the past and there has been enormous interest in and support for conservation. Several early gardens (notably Ham and Erddig) that were destroyed by Capability Brown or his imitators, or reconstructed in Victorian or Edwardian times, or lost to neglect, have had their original plans dug out of archives and muniment rooms and are being restored.

Whatever way it is, people seem ready for a change and are beginning to tire of the formless garden. Straight lines, clipped hedges, topiary and box are all making a comeback and once again there is a place in gardeners' hearts for the knot.

The court of the Old Palace seemed the ideal frame for a knot garden. It had high banks on three sides so that it could be looked down on, which, as we have seen, the knot gardens of the fifteenth and sixteenth centuries ideally were. It had water, was beautifully sheltered and did not seem to be a frost pocket. The creation of this garden was going to be fun, and I looked forward to it with keen anticipation. The first thing was to draw a plan. There were to be three knots and a foot maze, or labyrinth. Labyrinths, which may have originated in Crete or Egypt, featured in Tudor gardens as a relic of the Middle Ages. There are mazes on the floors of cathedrals and churches where sinful man, penitent, crawled round the labyrinth on his knees saying prayers at various stations on the way. Sometimes they were used as an alternative to going on a pilgrimage to the Holy Land, and were thought of as symbolizing man's journey through life, when, after transversing a tortuous and difficult path, he would finally reach Paradise. There is a story that Fair Rosamund Clifford, Henry II's mistress, hid in one to escape from Queen Eleanor, at whose hands she finally met her tragic fate.

At first glance, the court seemed to be square but measurement proved it otherwise, and when three square knots and a square labyrinth were fitted into the area, several empty spaces were left. These I filled with two long beds edged with winter savory (*Satureja montana*), and with the grey *Santolina chamaecyparissus* in the centres. In the other empty spaces, I put round beds, two each side of the entrance to the Palace, and planted a silver and golden variegated holly, topiaried in layers and underplanted with *Vinca minor* f. *alba* and *Scilla siberica*. The hedges of the knots and the labyrinth were of box, the plants being grown from thousands of cuttings raised in sand in 1979 and planted finger-sized in 1981, their root system much larger than their stem and leaf.

There were borders under the very low brick wall which had been the base of an openwork one, put in by the second Marquess in particularly ugly mauvish Victorian brick backed by a hoggin gravel path. We removed both borders and wall and planted whitethorn (*Crataegus laevigata* syn. *C. oxyacantha*), which was much used for clipped hedges in the fifteenth and sixteenth centuries, and we topiaried finials either side of the entrances to the garden. Old, probably seventeenth-century, bricks found on the estate were used to lay all the paths except the main cross paths. These, which are of York stone, had been put in by the fifth Marquess. They led to a round pond which I turned into a fountain with a limestone basin on a baluster supporting a single jet of water. In the paved circle around the fountain we put copies of Elizabethan terracotta pots, with a trellis pattern, which we planted with old varieties of clove carnations. There were now grass paths behind the whitethorn hedges at the bottoms of the grass banks, and at the top of the banks a low wooden trellis fence, which surrounded the whole garden, its posts crowned by wooden balls. These were coconut-shy balls found in a shop in Southampton!

What I believe is called the hard landscaping of the garden was now complete, and the treasure hunt for the plants began. Although the Palace was built in the late fifteenth century, I decided not to be too purist and limit myself to plants of that date, because I wanted also to include a collection of the plants introduced by the Tradescants and those grown up to 1700. Their colours, form and character seemed to look right, and to harmonize with the architecture and setting they grew in. Besides, many were rare and precious and needed to be in a place where they could be kept an eye on and, if necessary, propagated.

There were several people who gave me expert advice and shared with me their deep knowledge and experience in growing plants of these periods (not to speak of their generous gifts of the plants themselves) for which I shall always be grateful.

One was Roy Genders, whose books I had read and found to be a mine of precious information about early plants still surviving in gardens, their history and where they might be found. His delightful company I was lucky enough to enjoy on the several occasions he came to Hatfield to see the gardens, but more especially to talk about the plants grown in the gardens of Tudor and Stuart England, the florists' flowers, and those found in cottage gardens, many of which had survived in these gardens from the earliest times of their introduction, thanks to the cottagers faithfully propagating them from seeds and cuttings over the years. Among them were plants like the ancient pinks, the hose-in-hose cowslips and double primroses. Brian Halliwell, at Kew, was another erudite plantsman and botanist who came to see the garden while I was planting it and helped me greatly with his expertise and knowledge of early plants. Michael Hoog, who had a nursery in Haarlem where he grew rare and wonderful bulbs, many of which he had raised himself or found in the wild, also came to the garden and it was through him that the Hortus Bulborum in Holland sent me a collection of historic tulips and narcissus to grow there, including the swan-necked daffodil and the pink and white tulip 'Lac van Rijn' dating from 1620. These were all exciting acquisitions and added greatly to the interest in the garden.

John Harvey, with encyclopaedic knowledge of early plants, fruit and trees, produced a small book which was the inspiration of Maureen Taylor, the manager of our garden centre at Cranborne, listing all these plants with the descriptions of them and their dates of introduction. This was a great help to me as were my several visits to him and his wife at their home in Somerset.

Altogether I felt myself extremely fortunate to have the good help and support of such experts. Of course, the heat and burden of the day fell on the broad shoulders of Mr Beaumont and his team who carried out the construction of the garden and its planting in an impressively short time. It was begun in 1979 with the striking of box cuttings, and finished in 1982. The paths had been laid and the beds edged with bricks and the main planting had been completed. Remembering how much the Tudors and Elizabethans loved the bizarre and the fanciful, the striped, and the variegated, I planted the hedgehog holly and the plant like the skin of a snake, its leaves flesh-coloured with black, *Dracunculus vulgaris*, the dragon arum or snakeplant, also the rose root (*Rhodiola rosea*), hose-in-hose primroses, auriculas and double primroses, the great rose plantain with its green double leaf-like flowers and the plume hyacinth, as well as very many less eccentric plants, or plants not eccentric at all, like the Madonna lily, and the forget-me-not, which was the personal emblem of Henry of Lancaster, afterwards Henry IV, who wore it believing that those who did would never be forgotten.

I planted lavender, of course, which reached England with the Romans. William Lawson said that it was 'Good for bees', while Parkinson told us that 'It would pierce the senses . . . to comfort, and would dry up the moisture of a cold brain.' One hopes it worked. In 1579, Langham advises to 'boil it in water, wet thy shirt in it, dry it and wear it', and no doubt it would have helped those who seldom, if ever, took a bath, and those around them. In Elizabethan days a laundress was known as a 'lavendre'. Irises went in too, *germanica*, *pallida* and 'Florentina', also *Lilium chalcedonicum* with scarlet Turk's cap flowers which grew wild in the fields beyond Constantinople and was grown in every Tudor garden.

Candytuft, hyssop, thymes, *Matthiola longipetala* subsp. *bicornis*, the Elizabethan gardeners' night violet, with its delicious night-time scent, then gillofers or gillyflowers, which we call stocks. Hellebores too, and *Lychnis chalcedonica,* which was brought back by pilgrims at the time of the Crusades, with its tiny petals forming a scarlet cross, its English name being 'Cross of Jerusalem'. I planted as many of the pinks grown in those early times as I could find. Some were elusive, but as interest in them has grown over the last years, several have been rediscovered, including 'Nonsuch', 'Painted Lady' and 'Green Eyes' or 'Musgrave's Pink'.

Many bulbs were planted too, the Scottish crocus (*Crocus biflorus*), *Erythronium dens-canis*, *Colchicum autumnale* and snowdrops amongst them. Over the four bowers I had made, and set against the hedges facing north and south, I planted the sweetbriar (*Rosa rubiginosa),* the honeysuckle *Lonicera periclymenum*, and jasmine, which was first introduced in 1528, and used to form scented places to rest.

Roses of course, I have planted in abundance. Many, such as the Gallicas and Albas, can be traced back to classical times. The Damask roses were grown by the Persians, the Crusaders bringing them back to Europe, and Parkinson, in 1629, grew twelve different varieties. 'Alba Maxima' seems indestructible. It has lived for centuries in the gardens of castles and cottages, smells delicious, its flowers blush pink, turning to creamy white and 'double-double'. 'Alba Semiplena' was the white rose of York and then there is 'Maiden's Blush' called by the French 'Cuisse de Nymphe' or 'La Séduisante', names which give one a clue to its seductive beauty. *Rosa × centifolia*, the old cabbage rose, grown certainly before 1600, is double-double too, and a *rose des peintres* – another of its names, Redouté being one of the artists who painted it. A delicious little rose, a Gallica, 'Burgundiaca', the Burgundy Rose, only three feet high, with tiny flowers and leaves, I planted too. It is known to have been introduced before 1664. And the apothecary's rose, *R. gallica* var. *officinalis,* which has a romantic history. It is thought that the King of Navarre, who calls it in the poem 'the rose from the land of the Saracens' brought it to France in 1260 when returning from the Crusades. It has masses of crimson flowers gilded with golden stamens and a delectable scent. Then there is its sport *R. gallica* 'Versicolor', Rosa Mundi, Fair Rosamund's rose, with all the same delights as its parent, and almost as ancient. There are two Damask roses, 'Kazanlik' (*R. × damascena* 'Trigintipetala'), grown in Bulgaria to make attar of roses, and York and Lancaster (*R. × damascena* var. *versicolor*). This last, legend tells us, was the rose from which, during the Wars of the Roses, each side took a flower, one red, one white.

There is only one old rose that flowers repeatedly, rose 'De Rescht' with a scented flower of crimson-purple and probably with some Gallica blood. It was brought to England by Nancy Lindsay, in the 1920s or 1930s, from Iran, and nobody knows its real age. On the walls of the Palace, I planted *R. moschata*, the musk rose, very ancient and probably in England since the time of Elizabeth I. Its delicious scent pervades the air from August to the autumn.

The roses are planted in a *mélange* with other ancient plants, prominent amongst them the martagon lilies, a dusky pink growing abundantly with their white brothers. They are not only in the beds where I planted them but have seeded in the banks around the garden, as have the primroses and cowslips, and masses of ladies' bedstraw has appeared with its delicious scent of the freshest of new mown hay. I planted these banks with *Fritillaria meleagris*, Gerard's 'chequered daffodil', and possibly the flower in the line from Shakespeare's poem 'Venus and Adonis' – 'A purple flower chequered with white'. They flower in May, and with them *Muscari botryoides* 'Album', which came from Spain and could have been brought from there by Tradescant. It has a sweet scent, likened by Parkinson to 'starch when it is made new and hot'. Strangely, I cannot find any reference to the Elizabethans having grown the more common blue one, *M. botryoides*, the Italian grape hyacinth, although *M. racemosum* had naturalized itself in East Anglia in the sixteenth century.

When these banks are in full bloom with fritillaries, white grape hyacinths, cowslips and primroses, thick with their flowers, I find many a minute is lost gazing on them. For all the world they look like the flowering meadow of Botticelli's *Primavera*.

I had quite forgot to speak of the crown imperials I planted in the knots, a flower pictured in so many illustrations of gardens of the fifteenth and sixteenth centuries, said to have been given its name because it had first been grown in Europe by the Emperor of Austria. There are only two varieties, a red one and a yellow one, and they have never changed since their arrival from Persia and Turkey and their introduction to Europe by Clusius, who collected plants for the Emperor.

Francis Drake knew Clusius – and gave him plants from America – and the crown imperial was growing in several London gardens, and spoken of by Gerard, very soon after Drake's return from his voyage round the world in 1580. Shakespeare mentions it and Parkinson's *Paradisus terrestris* begins with praise of it. 'For its stately beautifulness deserveth the first place in this our garden of delight, to be here entreated of before all other lilies.'

If you turn up the flower, you will see teardrops within. They are perpetual, and nothing, neither shaking nor breaking, will dislodge them. It is said that it will for ever hold its tears, tears of shame, for failing to bow its head when Our Lord passed by.

After many years had gone by, the fountain from Italy became sadly decayed: it was irreparable and had to be replaced. There were other priorities and so the Knot Garden was disgraced by a drab-looking fountainless pool until 2001. At that time I was reading the *Hypnerotomachia Poliphili*, whose publication, as we have already seen, had had such a powerful influence on the art and design of gardens in the sixteenth and seventeenth centuries, when one of the drawings showing a boy standing on a sphere and blowing a trumpet struck me as being the perfect figure for the Knot Garden fountain. It had not only been drawn in the 1490s, very close to the date when the Old Palace was built, but had been designed for a garden. There was an exact description of how it was made. The boy had a hole in the back of his head and a wing below him. The wind caught the wing, which turned the figure, and then the wind entered the hole in his head and blew the trumpet. There was no description of the sort of sound it made, but one supposes it might have sounded somewhat like an Aeolian harp. What a challenge to create a fountain figure from a drawing and description over five hundred years old!

I decided to take up the challenge and got in touch with the expert and resourceful Mr Franklin, who had worked as organizer and manager of the works carried out at Hatfield by the Cambridge firm Rattee and Kett over thirty years or more. He gallantly came out of retirement to help, joining Mr Beaumont with his practical knowledge of almost every craft, Mr Tony Darwin, mason and man of many other skills, plus his mate Mr Alvin Shelsher, and Mr Wilson who fashioned reeds for the trumpet. Within something over a year, the octagon-shaped limestone fountain, made in China, was in place and the golden boy, complete with trumpet and wing, now reigns in gilded glory over the Palace garden. The sound from his trumpet is as yet only a faint whisper, but we are working on that, and what they achieved in 1492 surely can be accomplished with all the new technology of the twenty-first century: soon, I hope, a trumpet call will sound in the Knot when the wind blows.

I have now sung my swan songs in the gardens at Hatfield and I trust that my dream and vision over thirty years ago, that one day they might become as harmonious as a woman's face in the right hat, may have been, at least partially, fulfilled. A place planted with the deliciously fragrant homely plants which filled the gardens of the Tudors and Stuarts with sweetness and the hum of bees, and also a place of fancies and conceits, which would together fulfil the idea of a garden as a place where pleasure and peace are both to be found. We gardeners are continually reaching for a perfection that always seems to be just around the next corner and would wish to be like St Bernard almost ravished with the pleasures of it. 'A sick man' (saith he) 'sits upon a green bank, and when the dog-star parcheth the plains and dries up rivers, he lies in a shady bower,' (*Fronde sub arborea ferventia temperat astra*) 'and feeds his eye with variety of objects, herbs, trees, to comfort his misery, he receives many delightsome smells, and fills his ears with that sweet and various harmony of the birds. Good God,' (saith he) 'what a company of pleasures hast Thou made for man!'

ACKNOWLEDGEMENTS

The Dowager Marchioness of Salisbury

I would like to thank and make a special tribute to Sue Snell whose book this really is. My text merely accompanies her superb photographs which capture the essence and detail of the garden, its plants and, most importantly, those who work in it. Sue has been photographing the gardens at Hatfield for over seven years in every season and her observant and artistic eye has missed no detail in it worthy of her lens. The results are a truly remarkable record of a garden and its gardeners. I would like to thank, too, the Librarian at Hatfield House, Robin Harcourt Williams, who has patiently and efficiently supplied me with the information I needed from the archives, especially refreshing my memory with forgotten dates and details.

Without David Beaumont, the Head Gardener at Hatfield for getting on for twenty-five years, there would be no garden as depicted in Sue's photographs. Hours and holidays seem irrelevant to him. Apart from his family, the garden comes first with its animals and birds. Whether it is plants, flowers, trees, ornamental water fowl, wild life, pond life, dogs, sheep or deer, his encyclopaedic knowledge covers every aspect of them and their care. Like me, he is a convinced and dedicated organic gardener. He looked after my flock of black sheep and homeopathy was what they got when in need of medical treatment, which was seldom. His wife, Margaret Beaumont, has not only been a wonderful help in the garden, but is also a uniquely skilful arranger of delicious bouquets of flowers in the house. He and his team, Simon Scull, Larry Laird, Alan Purvis and Peter Baker and all present and past gardeners, outstanding students and those who went from Hatfield to headships (lucky employers who got a head gardener trained by Mr Beaumont!) have earned boundless gratitude for their work and dedication.

I would like, too, to thank the Henry Doubleday Research Association. I suppose I was one of its earliest supporters when Lawrence Hills first started it and from 1948 I have gardened organically. I have learnt much from them and also from the Soil Association and am grateful to both organizations who have done such admirable work for the environment.

I am sure I would not have been able to finish my history of the gardens on time if it had not been for the wonderful help of Elizabeth Dean. The task of deciphering my pencilled and untidy handwriting and typing it on her laptop she achieved incredibly swiftly. Her patience and humour never failed and I will for ever be grateful for this.

Finally, I would like to thank John Nicoll, my publisher, for his patience and understanding when I missed two deadlines, and Jo Christian, my editor, for her equal patience and kindness.

Sue Snell

A very big thank you to the Dowager Marchioness of Salisbury, to David and Margaret Beaumont, Larry and Eileen Laird, Robin Harcourt Williams, Elizabeth Dean, Joan Kendall and the Textile Conservators, and the Hatfield Archive and Estate including all the gardeners, staff and volunteers. Also to Valerie Finnis, Anne Jennings and the Museum of Garden History, Tiffany Daneff, Jess Walton, Marilee Kuhlmann, Metro Imaging, Peter Davies, Linda Melvern, Gwenda Saar, Georgina Warren, Linda Peryer, Sarah Raeburn, Shaun Romain and Wendy Robin. And finally to my agent, Anthea Morton-Saner at Curtis Brown, and her predecessor, Michael Shaw, to horticultural consultant Tony Lord, to the publisher, John Nicoll, the editor, Jo Christian, the designer, Becky Clarke, and the production controller, Caterina Favaretto.

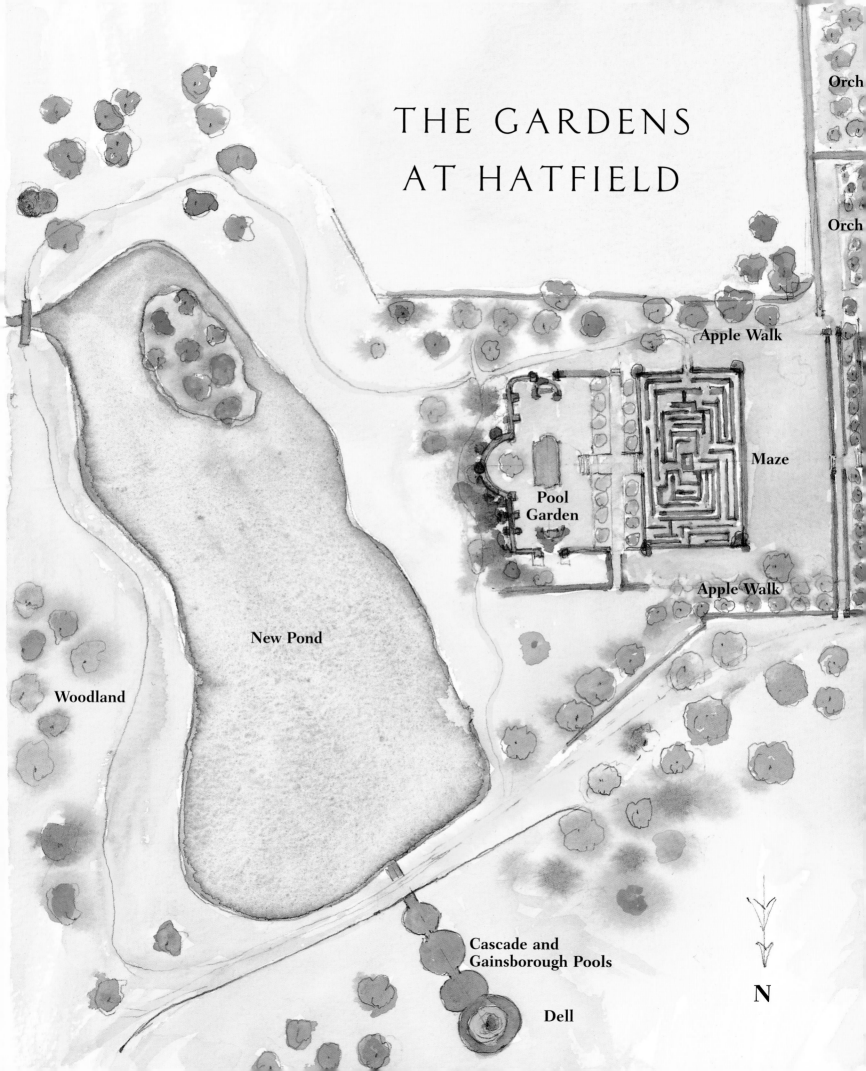

THE GARDENS AT HATFIELD

Orch

Orch

Apple Walk

Maze

Pool Garden

Apple Walk

New Pond

Woodland

Cascade and Gainsborough Pools

Dell

N

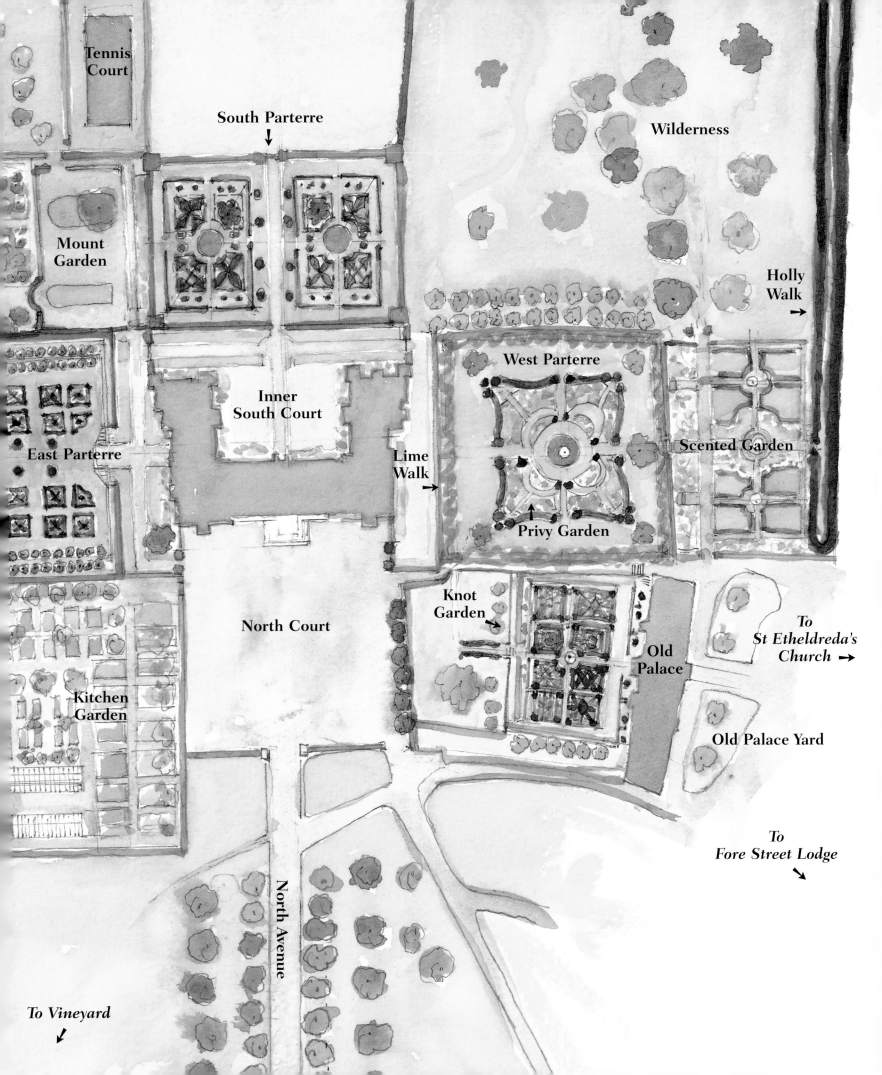

Tennis Court

South Parterre

Wilderness

Mount Garden

Holly Walk →

West Parterre

Inner South Court

Lime Walk →

Scented Garden

East Parterre

Privy Garden

Knot Garden

North Court

Old Palace

To St Etheldreda's Church →

Kitchen Garden

Old Palace Yard

To Fore Street Lodge ↘

North Avenue

To Vineyard ↓

NORTH

From the main gates, the approach to
Hatfield House is lined by the graceful beeches
(*Fagus sylvatica*) of the North Avenue.

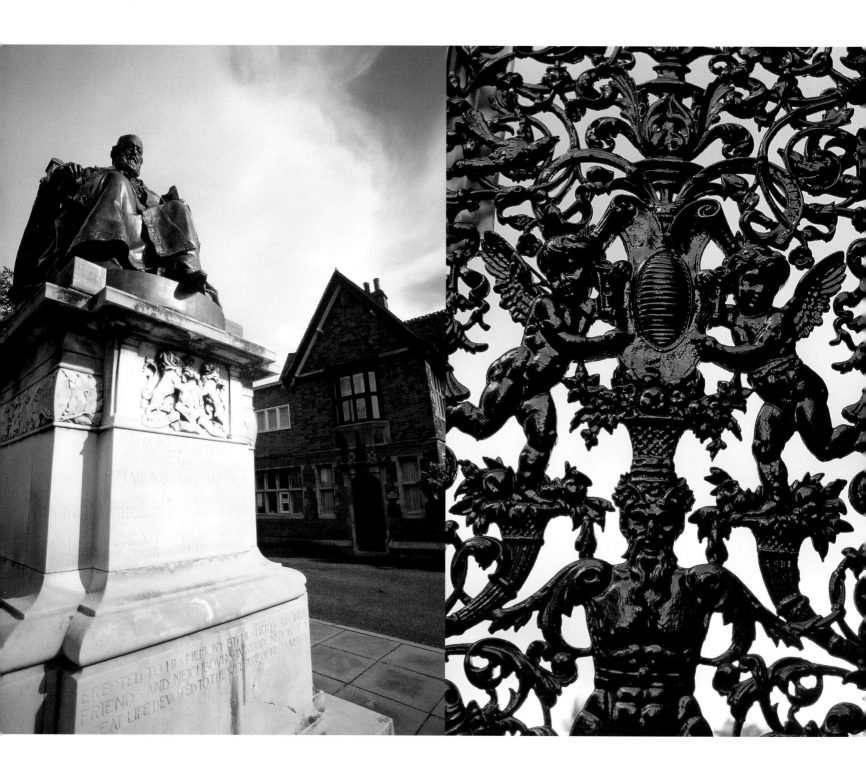

THE APPROACHES

Above left Across from the railway station is an imposing bronze statue by Sir George Frampton of the third Marquess of Salisbury (1830–1903).
Above right Ornate cast-iron gates mark the main entrance of Hatfield House.

Above left The wooden entry kiosk on the approach to
the house and park, backed by a yew hedge
Above right The stately beech avenue as it leads away
from the North Court towards the Parkland

THE NORTH COURT

From left to right The North Avenue, leading to the North Court and the main entrance with its impressive flight of steps rising to an oak door

FOLLOWING PAGES
Clockwise from top left A bust of the second Marquess (1791–1868) looks out on the rose 'Paul's Himalayan Musk'; a dove in flight; a detail of the fine cast-iron gates erected in 1846, which today house a dovecote in their supporting pillars; rose 'Saint Cecilia'; a metal plant label marking rose 'Cedric Morris'

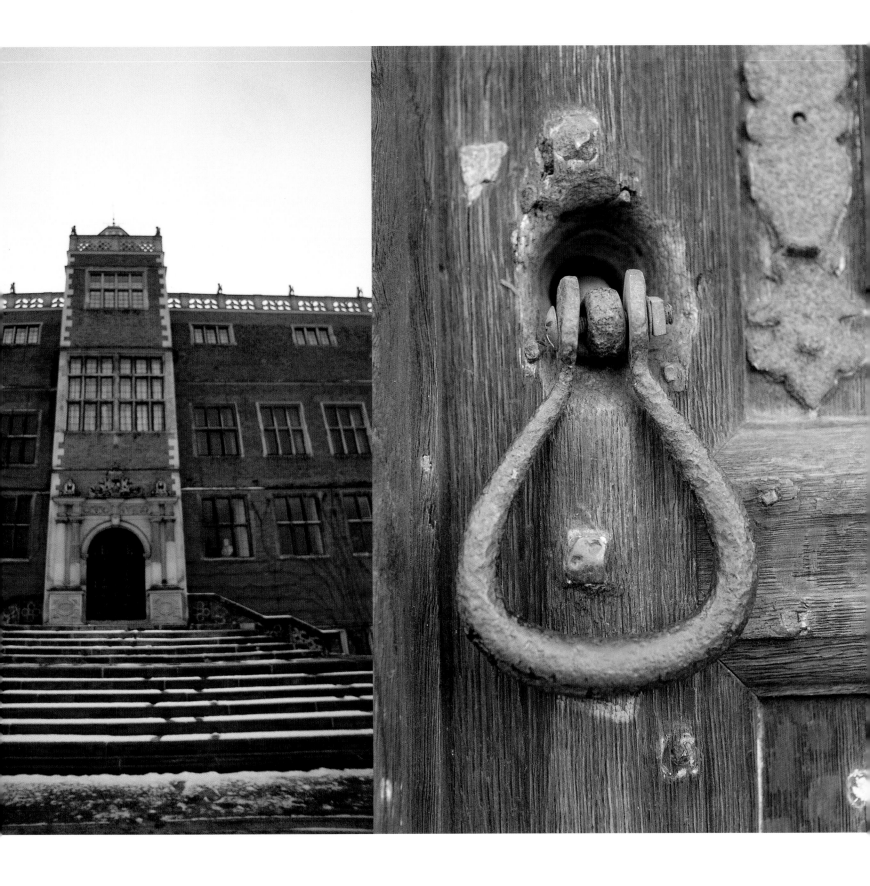

WEST

A view of the house from the Old Palace
Knot Garden. To the left is a great horse chestnut
(*Aesculus hippocastanum*), with a seat built
around its trunk; to the right is the Lime Walk,
leading to the Scented Garden.

THE OLD PALACE

Left, clockwise from top left The Banqueting Hall of the Old Palace, built in 1485 by John Morton, Bishop of Ely, and once home to Elizabeth I; the Fore Court entrance; a private road around the estate, bordered by hedging of hawthorn (*Crataegus monogyna*); visitors on their way to the restaurant for tea; *Rosa filipes* growing in the fleur-de-lys brick wall between St Etheldreda's church and the Old Palace; a hollyhock (*Alcea rosea*) in the garden
Right, above Rose 'Rambling Rector' rambles over the wall of the stable yard, *right* flowering in summer, *far right* in autumn
Right, below A commemorative plaque on the Old Palace wall

THE WEST PARTERRE

Far right *Phillyrea angustifolia* trees guard the
entrance to the West Parterre, with its Italian
eighteenth-century stone figures found by the
sixth Marquess and Marchioness at a villa near
Lake Como. The figures are framed by tall hedges
of yew and smaller box hedges.
Right, above A helmeted stone figure
accompanied by a lion, backed by yew hedges
and a holm oak (*Quercus ilex*)
Centre and below Details of the helmeted figure,
overlooking medlar trees (*Mespilus germanica*)

Left A view towards the house across box hedging clipped
to curve down then rise again to shaped finials
Centre An outcropping of the yew hedge, shaped as a
bower, enclosing a wooden seat shaded by a
walnut tree (*Juglans regia*)
Right Box hedging separating medlar trees from a path
leading to the Knot Garden of the Old Palace

THE KNOT GARDEN

Left and above The Old Palace, built in about 1485, and its Knot Garden. Created and planted by Lady Salisbury in 1982, the garden consists of three knots and a labryinth or foot maze, and includes plants known to have been grown between the fifteenth and seventeenth centuries. The fountain placed where two paths meet was designed by Lady Salisbury in 2004, after a drawing in the *Hypnerotomachia Poliphili*. High banks covered with native wild flowers and grasses enable the garden to be viewed from above.

FOLLOWING PAGES
Clockwise from top left The common almond (*Prunus dulcis*), on a bank of wild flowers and grasses; the cherry plum (*Prunus cerasifera*); the fountain with its gilded mobile boy complete with trumpet and wings, placed on a carved stone plinth; a stone boy on the steps up to the Old Palace; buttercups and other wild flowers above the Knot Garden; cherry trees in front of the Old Palace

Left The octagonal-patterned foot maze, in clipped box
Right, clockwise from top left
Oxeye daisies (*Leucanthemum vulgare*); cowslip (*Primula veris*); the majestic foxtail lily (*Eremurus*); the summer snowflake (*Leucojum aestivum*); pale yellow primroses (*Primula vulgaris*) with the snake's-head fritillary (*Fritillaria meleagris*)

Clockwise from above Rosa gallica var.
officinalis; two views of the black-tongued
dragon flower (*Dracunculus vulgaris*); cherry
pie (*Heliotropium arborescens*); a blue and
purple hyacinth (*Hyancinthus orientalis*);
a pink variety of lavender

FOLLOWING PAGES
The Lime Walk connects the Privy Garden
with the West Parterre and the Scented and
Wilderness Gardens, and forms an outer
edge to the West Parterre. The limes (*Tilia
platyphyllos*) are pleached each winter.
Spring flowers then bloom beneath until
the summer canopy takes over to form
shaded walkways.

THE LIME WALK

At the most westerly edge of the Lime Walk are two stone carvings by J.G. Bubb (1782–1853), taken from the façade of the Royal Exchange after a fire and brought to Hatfield in 1855. They have been placed in two arbours. Nearest to the Old Palace is Elizabeth I with her Court, including Lord Burghley. Further away is Britannia, seated amidst the emblems of Commerce and the Polite Arts.

THE PRIVY GARDEN

Left Lady Gwendolen Cecil, daughter of the third Marquess, designed this central garden. The yew hedges that enclose it are finished with clipped topiary finials. Each entrance is at one of the four main points of the compass.

Right, above Winter sun
and a sweet chestnut
(*Castanea sativa*)
Right, below A storm
brewing over Hatfield

FOLLOWING PAGES
Yew topiary and the canopy
of a sweet chestnut
framing the Privy Garden

Left Foxgloves, irises and roses in the Privy Garden
at mid-summer
Centre *Allium hollandicum* 'Purple Sensation' and
Euphorbia characias subsp. *wulfenii*
Right At the centre of this garden are brick-edged
herbaceous flower beds with detailed planting schemes,
arranged around a fountain.

The large stone pool of the fountain at the heart of the Privy Garden is home to white waterlilies (*Nymphaea alba*), golden carp and visiting mallard ducks.

A view from the Library of the West Parterre and the Privy Garden with its topiary, fountain and flowers. Through the gap in the trees can be seen Hatfield Old and New Towns. St Etheldreda's church is tucked behind the Old Palace.

Above, left to right Dodecatheon meadia;
Fritillaria pontica; Tulipa acuminata
Left Tulipa acuminata
Right Aquilegia formosa

FOLLOWING PAGES
Clockwise from top left Helleborus x
sternii; Scabiosa atropurpurea
'Ace of Spades'; *Viola* 'Bowles Black';
Aquilegia vulgaris var. *stellata;*
Iris 'Blackout'; *Iris* 'Radiant Apogee' with
Allium 'Purple Sensation'

Clockwise from top left
Paeonia peregrina; Crocus biflorus;
Muscari botryoides; Allium
hollandicum 'Purple Sensation'
with Euphorbia characias subsp.
wulfenii; a foxglove; Aquilegia
vulgaris var. stellata; Lobelia tupa

Left, clockwise from top left Mulberry (*Morus nigra*); rose 'Golden Wings'; the blossom of the medlar (*Mespilus germanica*); *Paeonia* 'Marie Crousse'; rose hips; medlar
Right, above The stained-glass window of the Chapel, dating from the early seventeenth century, depicts stories from the Bible. It was the work of Lewis Dolphin from France, Richard Butler of Southwark and Martin van Bentham from Holland.
Right, below Rose 'Kew Rambler' rambles across the Jacobean brickwork.

THE SCENTED GARDEN

Above Roses, sweet peas, jasmine, phlox and pinks perfume
the broad border in front of the wall that runs the
length of the western side of the Lime Walk.
Left, clockwise from top left A door set in the Old Palace wall
leading to steps and the door of the gardeners' bothy;
Rosa brunonii and honeysuckle (*Lonicera fragrantissima*)
climb around the bothy door; looking out over the
Scented Garden; inside the bothy

The Scented Garden with its stone-paved and gravel paths is bordered by three ancient brick walls, part of the Old Palace, and the clipped hedge of the Holly Walk. In the middle is the Herb Garden, with an eighteenth-century sundial at its centre. Honeysuckle, jasmine and roses clamber over the walls, and the beds are crammed full of scented plants, including lavender, *Perovskia* 'Blue Spire', the Hybrid Musk rose 'Kathleen', *Lilium regale*, sweet geraniums and the double pink 'White Ladies'.

Enter this garden by any number of gates and steps. Pass under elegant arches and find secret corners linked by paths. High box hedges formed into bowers over frames entice you to sit and enjoy the scents.

FOLLOWING PAGES
Left, clockwise from top left A tree peony; *Dianthus* 'Laced Monarch'; rose 'The Prince'; an old-fashioned red Rambler rose; rose 'Fritz Nobis'; rose 'Pretty Jessica'
Right Climbing rose 'Monsieur Delbard' scrambles over the wall separating the Scented Garden from the Wilderness.

Above The sunshine-yellow rose 'Graham Thomas'
Left, *above* 'Czar' plums, ripening and heavy,
bend their branches downwards.
Left, below All summer long droning bumble and
honey bees suck nectar from the lavender
and the other scented plants.

THE HOLLY WALK AND THE WILDERNESS

Left and above In reworking the Holly Walk Lady Salisbury was inspired by Borromini's Gallery in Perspective in the Spada Palace, Rome. The holly (*Ilex aquifolium)* columns are spaced so as to create an optical illusion, and the Walk appears much longer than it is in reality. Grassed, with stone edges, the Walk runs from north to south and catches the last rays of a setting sun. At one end is a limestone seat and at the other a carved head of Elizabeth I, set on a plinth. This carving, by J.G. Bubb, was also part of the façade of the Royal Exchange, and was brought to Hatfield in 1855.

FOLLOWING PAGES
The 13-acre Wilderness, which used to be the Shrubbery, runs alongside the Deer Park. Oaks, redwoods, beeches and birches tower over carpets of lily-of-the-valley, wild daffodils, hellebores, *Cyclamen hederifolium* and, in May, bluebells.

Left, clockwise from top left Prunus x yedoensis, underplanted
with wild daffodils (*Narcissus pseudonarcissus*); the great
sweet chestnut (*Castanea sativa*), possibly planted by Tradescant,
sadly lost in 2001; English bluebell (*Hyacinthoides non-scripta*);
Camellia 'Lady Alice'; *Magnolia kobus*
This page, clockwise from right A double narcissus; malus fruits;
rhododendron blossoms; *Helleborus* x *hybridus*;
the blossoms of *Acer platanoides* 'Crimson King'

SOUTH

Until about 1870 the main entrance to the house was on the south side. A walkway lined with half-standard holm oaks in ornate nineteenth-century containers leads to a further set of fine cast-iron gates, matching those on the north side and like them erected for Queen Victoria's visit in 1846. On either side of the path are parterres of box clipped to form stylized patterns – a Tudor rose, oak leaves, a shamrock and a fleur-de-lys.

PREVIOUS PAGES
Clockwise from top left The Deer Park: light fallow deer were reintroduced to the Park in the 1980s; mistletoe balls in the high trees; looking from the Outer South Court over the Inner Court towards the house, with the newly restored garden houses on either side; receding storm clouds over the walkway and the wintering holm oaks; each of the box parterres has a pool and fountain as its centrepiece; the South Court.

THESE PAGES
Plants in the Inner South Court
Left, top to bottom Tulipa 'White Parrot'; *Aquilegia* 'Iceberg'; *Fritillaria meleagris* subvar. *alba*
Right, clockwise from top Clematis 'Madame Baron-Veillard'; *Alcea rosea* 'Black Beauty'; the seedhead of pink *Paeonia delavayi*

Above left The private entrance to the house from the South Court.
Clematis montana 'Grandiflora' wreathes the window to the right of the
door. *Choisya* 'Aztec Pearl' is at the front of the bed on the other side.
Above right Rose-patterned wrought-iron gates link the Inner South
Court with the East Terrace and the West Terrace .
Left The corner of this bed beside the south front of the house is
marked by tiered topiary in variegated *Buxus* 'David Scott'. *Clematis*
'Madame Baron Veillard' and *Fuchsia magellanica* flourishes near by.
The magnolia on the wall behind has been here since at least the 1920s.

THE MOUNT GARDEN

Left An openwork nineteenth-century brick wall and a newly planted yew hedge
run between two of the garden houses.
Centre and right Another openwork wall, with 'Gerbe Rose' scrambling along and
through it, separates the Mount Garden from the East Parterre.

FOLLOWING PAGES
Clockwise from left The focus of the Mount Garden is a huge horse chestnut tree
(*Aesculus hippocastanum*) with a circular wooden seat built around it;
a bird box sited in an English oak (*Quercus robur*); the main mount gives views over
a wall to the nearby East Parterre; looking towards the Mount from the Orchard,
through an archway of beech.

EAST

The East Parterre in mid-summer. The box-edged
beds with their topiary centres billow with roses,
foxgloves, alliums, salvias and Oriental poppies.
Hidden between the beds and the avenues of
holm oak trees are early-eighteenth-century
stone statues found by Lady Salisbury in Italy.
They come from a villa near Lake Como.

THE EAST PARTERRE

Seventeenth-century Italian stone figures and a stone pineapple stand on the balustrading of the East Terrace above the East Parterre. To the right is a strawberry grape vine, *Vitis* 'Fragola'.

Left, clockwise from top left
Doves perching on a patterned
brick wall overshadowed by a
hawthorn hedge and the beautiful
tree *Paulownia fargesii*; racing
clouds and doves in flight over the
East Gardens; the view from King
James's Drawing Room over the
Terrace to the East Parterre and
beyond; another of the seventeenth-
century Italian stone figures,
entwined in *Wisteria sinensis*
Right A view from an upper floor
of the house of part of the East
Parterre with its topiary, towards
the yew Maze, the New Pond and
the woodland beyond

Left, clockwise from top left The East Parterre on a beautiful bleak
winter's day; a 'Conference' pear on the tree espaliered against
the wall below the balustrade; *Magnolia grandiflora*, beautiful in
flower and bud, growing against the house wall; an Italian figure
on the balustrade, with the espaliered pear tree below;
a pebblework star set into the path
Below left *Aquilegia vulgaris*
Below right The giant furry seedpods of *Wisteria sinensis*

FOLLOWING PAGES
Left A pebble star pointing the way through the yew topiary
to the small stone fountain directly below the figured
balustrade of the East Terrace
Right Clipped yew cylinders with tousled tops in winter snow,
and holm oaks with their clipped rounded lollipop heads

Clockwise from top left Scudding clouds pass over the New Pond behind an eighteenth-century Italian stone figure; in the box-edged beds box crowns offset plantings that include, here, *Wisteria venusta*; at the furthest corner from the house a small slipway leads under part of the decorative wall, through a wooden gate topped by the head of a stone cherub to the Kitchen Garden; *Rosa cerasocarpa* scrambles happily over and through a wall bordering the Box Walk; the path at the east end of the gardens leads to steps to the Box Walk.

Left The elegant Lily-flowered tulip 'China Pink'
Right A tree peony (a *Paeonia suffruticosa* cultivar) billows in profusion under the balustrade wall of the East Parterre, unfurling from fat, tight buds.

Left, clockwise from top left A dark
red peony which came from France
before the Second World War;
Helleborus x *hybridus*; *Helleborus*
Ashwood Garden Hybrid; *Tulipa*
'Arabian Mystery'
Right Tulipa 'Fantasy'

Left, above Zingy yellow *Euphorbia characias* subsp. *wulfenii*
Left, below left 'Brown Turkey' fig
Left, below right Erythronium 'Pagoda'
Right, clockwise from top left
Two-toned pink hollyhock (*Alcea rosea*); iridescent pale yellow *Paeonia* 'Mai Fleuri'; tricolour Langport iris 'Port'; an unnamed iris, given to Lady Salisbury by a friend; a sedum; *Nectaroscordum siculum*

Left and above Fragile, paper-thin Oriental poppies
– buds, flowers and seedheads

THE ORCHARD

Mown grass paths divide the
Orchard into sections, each planted
with apples, pears, gages, plums or
cherries, many of old varieties which
are carefully recorded on metal
labels. Espaliered apples form a
protective screen for peach trees.
The Orchard has also been home to
bees, and to Black Lambay Island
sheep, from Ireland.

Left David Beaumont, who has been Head Gardener at Hatfield for twenty-five years, surrounded by the fruits of the Orchard – apples, plums, quinces, almonds and pears
Right Larry Laird trimming the beech hedge around the Orchard

FOLLOWING PAGES
The Maze was created in yew (*Taxus baccata*) in 1841. At its centre one yew tree has been trained to create two lions. The Maze is painstakingly clipped once a year, in summer, by Larry Laird. Using an electric hedge-cutter, he can complete the job within three weeks.

THE APPLE WALKS

Left On either side of the Maze are the Apple Walks. The apples are all old varieties, many originating as far back as the sixteenth and seventeenth centuries. By late summer the trees are laden with fruit. Roses scramble over the enclosing walls and ducks from the New Pond come here to search out food.
Right Mulberries, pears and apples. The gathered apples (*bottom right*) are 'Coeur de Boeuf' and 'Lord Derby'.

THE POOL GARDEN

Far left, above David Beaumont picking apples in autumn by the steps leading from the Box Walk to the East Parterre
Left, above Autumn windfalls in the Pool Garden
Far left, below Below the Maze, in the Pool Garden, there is another avenue of apple trees.
Left, below A stone statue of a man, carved by Hamish Horsley, stands close to the yew hedge of the Maze.
Right, above and below A twelve-foot-high yew hedge, furnished with buttresses, ensures seclusion for the Pool Garden.

THE WOODLAND

At the entrance to the Woodland an archway of purple beech (*Fagus sylvatica*) links the yew hedges. Beyond, a mixed planting of trees – from ancient beeches to young crab apples – is underplanted with a carpet of daffodils and hellebores.

THE NEW POND AND THE DELL

The New Pond may be on the site of the long-lost Great Water Parterre, designed by the water engineer and architect Salomon de Caus in the early seventeenth century.

Left The New Pond is home to numerous species of ducks, geese, swans and other water birds.

Below On the side of the pond nearest the house are large sunken plastic containers of waterlilies (*Nymphaea alba*).

Right, above In the area between the pond and the garden tall purple beech trees (*Fagus sylvatica*) and Daimio oaks (*Quercus dentata*) provide structure.

Far right, above The ruin of the front façade, complete with doorway, of the Elizabethan manor house Wood Hall conceals a boathouse.

Right, below The grass and wild flowers grow high until they are mown in August.

Far right, below The Apple Walk running up between the Maze and the Woodland, after mowing

Left, clockwise from top The blossom of the cherry plum, *Prunus cerasifera*; frosted oak leaves in the undergrowth; tiny *Cyclamen hederifolium* peeping through fallen autumn leaves
Right, clockwise from top Snake's-head fritillaries (*Fritillaria meleagris*) carpet the Woodland; elderberries (*Sambucus nigra*); pond-side purple loosestrife (*Lythrum salicaria*)

FOLLOWING PAGES
In her last year at Hatfield Lady Salisbury transformed the Dell by creating the Cascade and the Gainsborough Pools, inspired by a Gainsborough landscape. First a fence was moved back towards the Park and hard-working Tamworth pigs cleared the ground; then, under David Beaumont's supervision, the four interconnecting circular pools were dug. The largest, 48 feet wide, has a holm oak at its centre.

THE KITCHEN GARDEN

Lady Salisbury has always been committed to organic gardening, never using artificial pesticides or chemicals. She also mixes flowers with vegetables and fruit, as the Tradescants did, and uses companion planting. In the Kitchen Garden the Chinese deep bed system is used: the 'no-dig' narrow beds are mulched with organic matter. Making compost (*left*) is essential. The cloches (*far right*) are from Thailand, where they are used for cockfighting; here they are useful for keeping pigeons off young vegetable plants.

Left to right The late-nineteenth-century wrought-iron gates between the East Parterre and the Kitchen Garden; asparagus, which is cut to eat and also used for flower arrangements in the house; apples trained over metal frames, forming covered walkways that lead to a brick pool; and an Italian stone fountain encased by a box hedge

Left, above The eastern part of the Kitchen Garden, seen from the wooden seat next to the gate from the East Parterre

Left, below A polytunnel offering protection for tender plants and seedlings

Right, above The Kitchen Garden in summer
Right, below Polytunnels are used to toughen up vegetable and salad seedlings and encourage young plants to grow on.

The potting shed
and gardeners' hut

Left, above On either side of the greenhouse are two large water tanks copied from a seventeenth-century design. They contain water plants including (*left*) water soldier (*Stratiotes aloides*) and are sometimes used to root plants – such as the cornus just visible under the water in the tank *far left* – which are going to grow near water.

Left, below Indoor plants for the house, being nurtured in the greenhouse; lettuce seedlings in one of the polytunnels

Right, top to bottom A potato flower; artichokes (*Cynara cardunculus* Scolymus Group), which are cut for flower arrangements for the house; black kale

Above Sunshine in the Kitchen Garden: the fruits and flowers of
courgette 'Gold Rush', and the yellow-stalked chard 'Harlequin'

FOLLOWING PAGES
Left, clockwise from top left 'Cox's Orange Pippin' apple; 'Onward' pear;
'Harlequin' chard; 'Malling Admiral' raspberries; 'Victoria' plums
Right, clockwise from top left 'Red Lake' redcurrants; the flowers of
runner bean 'Scarlet Emperor'; 'White Versailles' figs; a flower bud of
the night-flowering Queen of the Night cactus (*Selenicereus
grandiflorus*); a 'Brandywine' tomato

Left, clockwise from far left Dark-hued globe artichoke 'Violetto di Chioggia'; red cabbage; beetroot 'Detroit 2' *Right* Red cabbage (*above*) and Brussels sprout 'Rubine'

THE PARK

Hatfield's 56 acres of gardens are surrounded by about 7,000 acres of parkland.

Above, left and right Ancient oaks (*Quercus robur*)
Left, below Mixed woodland
Right, below The North Avenue, lined with lime trees (*Tilia platyphyllos*)

Above These old gnarled and hollowed-out oaks
are survivors from before the time of Robert
Cecil.
Right A variety of fungi (most of it poisonous)
can be found in the Park.

THE VINEYARD

The Vineyard with its central gatehouse leads from the Park to the river. The walls of the Vineyard (*right, above*) were built in 1633. Today there are only token vines: instead (*left, below*) hedges of yew (*Taxus baccata*) frame the entrance and (*right, below*) the mown grass walkways are edged with *Thuja plicata*.

Left Views of the Vineyard and the river
Right Peacocks, peahens and chickens, together with an owl carving by Larry Laird, adorn this private and secluded area.

PLANT LISTS

APPROACHES AND NORTH COURT
Azara lanceolata
Cytisus x *praecox*
Lamium galeobdolon
Phillyrea latifolia
Prunus glandulosa 'Alba Plena'
Rosa 'Paul's Himalayan Musk';
   R. 'St Cecilia'
Tolmiea menziesii 'Taff's Gold'

WEST PARTERRE AND PRIVY GARDEN
Acaena saccaticupula 'Blue Haze'
Acanthus mollis
Actaea simplex Atropurpurea Group
Alcea rosea
Allium hollandicum 'Purple Sensation';
   A. karataviense
Alstroemeria
Aquilegia vulgaris var. *stellata*;
   A. formosa; *A. nevadensis*;
   A. scopulorum
Arabis ferdinandi-coburgi 'Old Gold'
Astrantia major subsp. *involucrata*
   'Shaggy'
Brachyglottis (Dunedin Group)
   'Moira Red'
Buxus sempervirens
Campanula garganica 'Dickson's Gold'
Castanea sativa
Crataegus monogyna
Crocus biflorus
Dahlia merckii
Dicentra eximia
Digitalis sibirica
Dodecatheon meadia
Eomecon chionantha
Eremurus himalaicus, fringed
Erysimum 'Bowles Mauve'; *E.* 'Constant
   Cheer'; *E.* 'Jacob's Jacket'; *E.* 'Jubilee
   Gold'; *E.* 'Orange Flame'; *E.* 'Sprite'
Euphorbia amygdaloides 'Variegata';
   E. characias subsp. *wulfenii*;
   E. x *martini*
Fritillaria pontica
Geranium clarkei 'Kashmir White';
   G. x *oxonianum* 'Wargrave Pink';
   G. x *oxonianum* 'Southcombe Star';
   G. phaeum 'Variegatum';
   G. sanguineum 'Compactum';
   G. sessiliflorum subsp.
   novae-zelandiae 'Nigricans'
Hebe 'Hagley Park'
Helianthemum 'Fire Dragon';
   H. 'Henfield Brilliant';
   H. 'Mrs C.W. Earle'; *H.* 'Wisley Primrose'
Helleborus foetidus Wester Flisk Group;
   H. x *hybridus* 'Libre'; *H.* x *sternii*;
   H. x *s.* 'Boughton Beauty'
Heuchera cylindrica 'Greenfinch';
   H. micrantha var. *diversifolia*
   'Palace Purple'
Ipheion
Iris 'Anniversary' (Siberian); *I.* 'Blackout';
   I. 'Cantab' (Reticulata); *I.* 'Fourfold
   White' (Siberian); *I.* 'Indeed'
   (Intermediate Bearded); *I.* 'Joyce'
   (Reticulata); *I.* 'Limeheart' (Siberian);
   I. 'Radiant Apogee'

Juglans regia
Lamium maculatum 'White Nancy'
Lavatera x *clementii* 'Rosea'
Lobelia tupa
Lysimachia ephemerum
Malva sylvestris 'Primley Blue'
Marrubium cylleneum 'Velvetissimum'
Mespilus germanica
Morus nigra
Muscari botryoides
Myosotis scorpioides 'Mermaid'
Nymphaea alba
Oenothera macrocarpa
Othonna cheirifolia
Paeonia lactiflora 'Doctor Alexander
   Fleming'; *P. lactiflora* 'Karl
   Rosenfield'; *P.* 'Marie Crousse';
   P. peregrina
Penstemon 'Alice Hindley';
   P. 'Burgundy;' *P.* 'Edithae';
   P. hirsutus var. *pygmaeus*; *P. jamesii*;
   P. 'Sour Grapes'
Persicaria campanulata
Phlomis chrysophylla
Phillyrea angustifolia
Phygelius aequalis 'Yellow Trumpet';
   P. x *rectus* 'African Queen';
   P. x *r.* 'Salmon Leap'
Physostegia virginiana var. *speciosa*
   'Variegata'
Primula vulgaris subsp. *sibthorpii*;
   P. wilsonii var. *anisodora*
Prunus rhexii
Quercus ilex
Rhodanthemum hosmariense
Romneya coulteri
Rosa 'Ballerina'; *R.* 'Golden Wings';
   R. 'Kew Rambler'
Salvia interrupta; *S. uliginosa*
Saxifraga 'Dr Wells'; *S.* 'Golden Falls'
Scabiosa atropurpurea 'Ace of Spades'
Sphaeralcea fendleri
Stachys macrantha 'Superba'
Taxus baccata
Teucrium chamaedrys 'Variegatum';
   T. scorodonia 'Crispum Marginatum'
Tradescantia (Andersoniana Group)
   'Osprey'
Trollius x *cultorum* 'Alabaster'
Tulipa acuminata; *T.* 'Cape Cod';
   T. 'Greenland'; *T.* 'Kansas';
   T. 'Purissima'; *T.* 'Queen of Night'
Verbascum olympicum
Veronica gentianoides
Viola 'Bowles Black'

LIME WALK
Anemone appennina; *A. blanda*;
   A.b. 'White Beauty'; *A. coronaria*;
   A. De Caen Group
Dodecatheon meadia f. *album*
Epimedium x *rubrum*
Galanthus nivalis
Galium odoratum
Helleborus cosmos; *H.* x *hybridus*;
   H. x *h.* 'Nancy Ballard'; *H.* x *h.* 'Sylvia';
   H. niger 'Potter's Wheel'; *H. orientalis*
   subsp. *guttatus*; *H. viridis*
Heuchera
Parahebe catarractae

Polygonatum x *hybridum*
Puschkmia scilloides var. *libanotica*
Ranunculus ficaria 'Brazen Hussy'
Tilia platyphyllos   -
Vinca

KNOT GARDEN
Buxus sempervirens 'Suffruticosa'
Crataegus laevigata
Helleborus foetidus
Hemerocallis fulva
Iris latifolia; *I. xiphium*
Jasminum
Lathyrus vernus
Lavandula
Lonicera periclymenum
Mandragora officinarum
Muscari botryoides 'Album';
   M. comosum 'Plumosum'
Narcissus odorus 'Double Campernelle'
Paliurus spina-christi
Plantago major 'Rosularis'
Primula (doubles, Jack-in-the greens,
   hose-in-hose)
Prunus cerasifera; *P. dulcis*; *P. rhexii*
Rhodiola rosea
Santolina chamaecyparissus
Sedum acre 'Aureum'
Teucrium fruticans
Tulipa saxatilis

ROUND BEDS
Aquilegia canadensis
Crocus biflorus
Ilex 'Silver Queen'
Lotus corniculatus 'Plenus'
Lychnis chalcedonicum
Primula vulgaris (double); *P. marginata*;
   P. 'Wanda'; *P.* 'White Wanda'
Rosa 'Alba Maxima';
   R. x *damascena* var. *versicolor*;
   R. gallica var. *officinalis*;
   R. g. 'Versicolor'; *R.* 'Maiden's Blush'
Scilla siberica
Tulipa 'Lac van Rijn'
Vinca minor f. *alba*

KNOTS
Althaea officinalis
Amsonia tabernaemontana
Aquilegia vulgaris var. *stellata* (red-
   flowered); *A. vulgaris* var. *flore-pleno*
Artemisia absinthium
Aruncus dioicus
Asphodelus luteus
Aster tradescantii
Campanula persicifolia
Clematis recta
Delphinium elatum
Dianthus (in variety)
Dracunculus vulgaris
Fritillaria imperialis
Genista tinctoria
Geranium pratense 'Striatum'
Gladiolus murielae
Helleborus niger
Hesperis matronalis
Hyssopus officinalis 'Roseus'
Iris 'Florentina'; *I. germanica*; *I. pallida*
Lavandula stoechas subsp. *pedunculata*
Leucojum aestivum

Lilium candidum; *L. martagon*
Lotus hirsutus
Lunaria rediviva
Lychnis viscaria
Matthiola longipetala subsp. *bicornis*
Monarda didyma
Omphalodes verna
Paeonia mascula
Phillyrea angustifolia; *P. decora*;
   P. latifolia
Ranunculus aconitifolus 'Flore Pleno';
   R. acris 'Flore Pleno'
Salvia sclarea
Santolina pinnata subsp. *neapolitana*;
   S. rosmarinifolia
Sedum acre; *S. telephium*
Silene dioica 'Flore Pleno'
Stachys germanica
Teucrium fruticans
Verbascum phoeniceum

SIDE BORDERS
Achillea tomentosa
Aconitum napellus; *A. napellus*
   Anglicum Group
Actaea rubra; *A. pachypoda*
Amaryllis belladonna
Anemone x *fulgens*
Aquilegia vulgaris (cottage double pink)
Artemisia abrotanum
Arum italicum
Atriplex halimus
Ballota pseudodictamnus
Chamaemelum nobile 'Flore Pleno'
Cardamine pratensis 'Flore Pleno'
Coronilla valentina
Crocus biflorus
Cyclamen coum subsp. *coum*
   f. *pallidum* 'Album'
Daphne mezereum
Dictamnus albus var. *purpureus*
Digitalis ferruginea; *D. grandiflora*;
   D. lutea
Eryngium alpinum
Erythronium dens-canis
Fragaria moschata (female and male);
   F. vesca 'Fructu Albo';
   F. vesca 'Muricata'
Fritillaria meleagris
Galanthus nivalis
Geranium phaeum
Helianthemum nummularium
Rosa 'Alba Semiplena'; *R.* 'Burgundiaca';
   R. x *centifolia*; *R.* x *damascena*
   'Trigintipetala'

SCENTED GARDEN
BORDERS
Abeliophyllum distichum
Buddleja x *weyeriana* 'Potneys Gold'
Calamintha grandiflora
Chimonanthus fragrans
Daphne x *burkwoodii*; *D. mezereum*
   f. *alba*; *D. odora* 'Aureomarginata';
   D. tangutica
Dianthus 'Laced Monarch';
   D. 'White Ladies'
Elaeagnus commutata; *E.* 'Quicksilver'
Geranium macrorrhizum 'Czakor'
Iris reticulata
Lathyrus odoratus

Lavandula lanata; L. stoechas
Lilium auratum; L. regale
Lonicera fragrantissimum; L. standishii
Melianthus major
Narcissus
Nepeta camphorata; N. govaniana;
 N. nuda; N. sibthorpii
Oenothera odorata
Osmanthus x burkwoodii
Ozothamnus ledifolius
Pelargonium (scented, in variety)
Perovskia atriplicifolia; P. 'Blue Spire'
Philadelphus coronarius 'Variegatus';
 P. 'Mont Blanc'
Phlomis italica
Ptelea trifoliata
Rhododendron 'Dora Amateis'
Ribes odoratum
Rosa 'Fritz Nobis'; *R.* 'Graham Thomas';
 R. 'Kathleen'; *R.* 'Pretty Jessica'
Salvia aucheri; S. candelabrum; S. repens
Sarcococca hookeriana var. *humilis*
Syringa x laciniata;
 S. pubescens subsp. *microphylla*
Tulipa 'Prince of Austria';
 T. 'Prince of Orange'
Viburnum x bodnantense;
 V. x carlcephalum; V. carlesii 'Aurora';
 V. farreri; V. x juddii
Viola odorata

WALLS
Aloysia triphylla
Buddleja auriculata
Calycanthus occidentalis
Chimonanthus praecox
Clematis 'Apple Blossom';
 C. macropetala; C. montana
 var. *wilsonii; C.* 'Sylvia Denny'
Coronilla valentina subsp. *glauca*
 'Variegata'
Clerodendrum trichotomum
Jasminum beesianum; J. officinale;
 J. officinale 'Aureum';
 J. x stephanense
Lonicera caprifolium; L. periclymenum
 'Belgica'
Trachelospermum asiaticum;
 T. jasminoides;
 T. jasminoides 'Variegatum'
Rosa brunonii; R. 'Kathleen';
 R. 'Monsieur Delbard'
Wisteria venusta; W. sinensis

HERB GARDEN
Allium cepa; A. fistulosum; A. moly
Anthriscus cerefolium
Artemisia abrotanum
Chicorum intybus
Cydonia oblonga
Cynara cardunculus Scolymus Group
Foeniculum vulgare 'Purpureum'
Helichrysum italicum
Hyssopus officinalis (pink, blue
 and white)
Iris latifolia; I. pallida
Isatis tinctoria
Levisticum officinale
Lonicera periclymenum 'Belgica'
Melissa officinalis

Mentha x piperita; M. spicata;
 M. suaveolens 'Variegata';
 M. x villosa
Myrrhis odorata
Origanum onites; O. vulgare;
 O. v. 'Aureum'; *O. v.* subsp. *hirtum*
Persicaria bistora
Rosmarinus var. *angustissimus*
 'Benenden Blue'; *R. officinalis;*
 R. o. 'Aureus'; *R. o.* 'Primley Blue';
 R. o. 'Roseus'
Rumex acetosa
Ruta graveolens 'Variegata'
Salvia officinalis 'Icterina';
 S. o. 'Purpurescens';
 S. o. 'Tricolor'
Sanguisorba minor
Santolina rosmarinifolia
Satureja montana
Sium sisarum
Tanacetum balsamita;
 T. vulgare var. *crispum*
Thymus (in variety)
Tropaeolum majus
Viola odorata

THE WILDERNESS
Acer 'Aureovariegatum'; *A. circinatum;*
 A. griseum; A. japonicum;
 A. negundo 'Flamingo'
Amelanchier x grandiflora 'Ballerina';
 A. lamarckii
Araucaria araucana
Arbutus andrachnoides; A. menziesii;
 A. unedo
Betula
Camellia 'Cornish Snow'; *C.* 'Lady Alice'
Cedrus libani
Cercidiphyllum japonicum
Clethra alnifolia
Convallaria majalis
Cornus alternitifolia 'Argentea';
 C. mas 'Aurea'
Corylopsis glabrescens; C. pauciflora;
 C. sinensis var. *calvescens* f. *veitchiana*
Cotinus 'Flame';
 C. coggygria 'Royal Purple'
Crataegus persimilis 'Prunifolia';
 C. wattiana
Cyclamen hederifolium
Davidia involucrata; D. i. var. *vilmoriniana*
Desfontainia spinosa
Disanthus cercidifolius
Enkianthus campanulatus; E. cernus
 f. *rubens; E. perulatus; E. chinensis*
Eucalyptus gunnii;
 E. pauciflora subsp. *niphophila*
Eucryphia x intermedia 'Rostrevor';
 E. x nymansensis; E. x nymansensis
 'Mount Usher'; *E. x n.* 'Nymansay'
Fagus 'Rohanii'; *F. sylvatica* var.
 heterophylla f. *laciniata; F.* 'Zlatia'
Fothergilla gardenii; F. major
Fraxinus excelsior 'Jaspidea'
Helleborus (in variety)
Halesia carolina; H. monticola;
 H. monticola var. *vestita*
Hoheria glabrata; H. sexstylosa
Hyacinthoides hispanica; H. non-scripta
Koelreuteria paniculata

Lespedeza japonica 'Albiflora';
 L. thunbergii
Ligustrum lucidum
 'Excelsum Superbum'
Lomatia myricoides
Magnolia campbellii subsp.
 mollicomata; M. kobus; M. x loebneri
 'Merrill'; *M. x proctoriana;*
 M. stellata; M. wilsonii
Malus x zumi 'Golden Hornet'
Metasequoia glyptostroboides
Narcissus pseudonarcissus
Nothofagus x alpina; N. antarctica;
 N. dombeyi; N. obliqua
Ostrya carpinifolia
Oxydendron arboreum
Parrotia persica
Photinia beauverdiana
Prunus 'Hally Jolivette'; *P.* 'Pink Shell';
 P. sargentii; P. 'Snow Goose';
 P. x yedoensis 'Shidare-yoshino'
Quercus cerris; Q. coccinea; Q. frainetto;
 Q. ilex; Q. petraea; Q. robur
Rhododendron augustinii
Robinia hillierii; R. hispida
 'Macrophylla'; *R. kelseyi;*
 R. pseudoacacia; R. p. 'Bessoniana';
 R. p. 'Frisia'
Stewartia malacondendon Koreana
 Group; *S. monadelpha; S. ovata* var.
 grandiflora; S. pseudocamellia
Styrax japonicus
Ulmus 'Sapporo Autumn Gold'
Viburnum betulifolium; V. x burkwoodii
 'Park Farm Hybrid'; *V. cylindricum*
Zelkova serrata 'Village Green'
Zenobia pulverulenta

SOUTH COURT
Alcea rosea 'Black Beauty'
Aquilegia 'Iceberg'
Buxus 'David Scott';
 B. sempervirens 'Suffruticosa'
Choisya 'Aztec Pearl'
Clematis 'Madame Baron-Veillard';
 C. montana 'Grandiflora'
Fritillaria meleagris subvar. *alba*
Fuchsia magellanica
Magnolia denudata
Paeonia delavayi
Phillyrea angustifolia; P. latifolia
Quercus ilex
Taxus baccata
Tulipa 'White Parrot'

EAST PARTERRE
SIDE BORDERS
Aquilegia 'Anne Calder';
 A. buergeriana; A. vulgaris
Buddleja fallowiana
Carex oshimensis 'Evergold'
Ceratostigma plumbaginoides
Clematis connata; C. chrysocoma;
 C. 'Kermesina'; *C. montana*
Euphorbia characias subsp. *wulfenii;*
 E. 'Gold Burst'; *E. myrsinites*
Fremontodendron californicum
Geranium lambertii; G. renardii;
 G. traversii var. *elegans*
Hebe 'Glaucophylla Variegata'

Helleborus atrorubens; H. Ashwood
 Garden hybrid; *H. x hybridus*
Hippocrepis emerus
Iris foetidissima 'Variegata';
 I. 'Nylon Ruffles'; *I.* 'Port'
Lavatera x clementii 'Barnsley'
Lonicera x brownii 'Dropmore Scarlet'
Magnolia grandiflora
Malus toringo subsp. *sargentii*
Margyricarpus pinnatus
Ophiopogon planiscapus 'Nigrescens'
Oxalis articulata 'Alba'
Paeonia mlokosewitschii; P. suffruticosa
Paulownia fargesii
Quercus ilex
Rosa 'Albéric Barbier'; 'Cécile Brünner';
 R. cerasocarpa; R. 'Oeillet Parfait';
 R. 'Louis XIV'
Salvia involucrata 'Bethellii'
Syringa meyeri 'Palibin'
Tanacetum haradjanii
Taxus baccata
Tropaeolum speciosum
Viburnum corylifolium
Vitis 'Fragola'
Wisteria sinensis; W. s. 'Alba'

CENTRE BEDS
Alcea rosea
Buddleja x weyeriana 'Potneys Gold'
Buxus sempervirens 'Suffruticosa'
Campanula persicifolia
Cistus crispus; C. cyprius;
 C. x dansereaui 'Decumbens';
 C. x hybridus
Dianthus (in variety)
Diascia fetcaniensis
Digitalis
Eryngium planum
Erythronium 'Pagoda'
Euphorbia (in variety)
Halimiocistus wintonensis
Hebe 'Edinensis'
Helleborus (in variety)
Hepatica transsilvanica
Kolkwitzia amabilis
Lilium (in variety)
Lysimachia ephemerum
Nectaroscordum siculum
Oenothera acaulis
Papaver orientale; P. o. 'Perry's White'
Paeonia 'Mai Fleuri'; *P. rockii*
Phygelius aequalis 'Yellow Trumpet'
Potentilla suffruticosa 'Princess'
Ribes laurifolium
Salvia forsskaolii
Tulipa 'Arabian Mystery'; *T.* 'China Pink';
 T. 'Fantasy'
Wisteria venusta

NEW POND AND DELL
Cyclamen hederifolium
Fagus sylvatica
Fritillaria meleagris
Lythrum salicaria
Nymphaea alba
Prunus cerasifera
Quercus dentata
Sambucus nigra

INDEX Page numbers in *italics* refer to captions to the illustrations